India's National Security:
A Maritime Security Perspective

India's National Security:
A Maritime Security Perspective

Editor

Dr SURESH R.

Professor & Hon. Director
V K Krishna Menon Study Centre for International Relations,
Department of Political Science,
University of Kerala,
Kariavattom Campus, Thiruvananthapuram,
Kerala State

Published in Association with
V K Krishna Menon Study Centre for International Relations,
University of Kerala, Thiruvananthapuram

Vij Books India Pvt Ltd

New Delhi (India)

Published by

Vij Books India Pvt Ltd
(Publishers, Distributors & Importers)
2/19, Ansari Road
Delhi – 110 002
Phones: 91-11-43596460, 91-11-47340674
Mob: +91-98110 94883
e-mail: contact@vijpublishing.com
web: www.vijbooks.com

Copyright © 2020, *Suresh R.*

First Published : 2020

ISBN: 978-93-89620-07-8 (PB)

ISBN: 978-93-89620-08-5 (ebook)

All rights reserved.

No part of this book may be reproduced, stored in a retrieval system, transmitted or utilized in any form or by any means, electronic, mechanical, photocopying, recording or otherwise, without the prior permission of the copyright owner. Application for such permission should be addressed to the publisher.

The views expressed in this book are those of the contributors in their personal capacity. These do not have any official endorsement.

Contents

Contributors

1. **Vice Admiral M P Muralidharan, AVSM, NM (Retd)** was Former Director General, Indian Coast Guard.

2. **Dr Suresh R**, Professor & Hon. Director, V K Krishna Menon Study Centre for International Relations, Department of Political Science, University of Kerala, Kariavattom Campus, Thiruvananthapuram, Kerala.

3. **N Sathiya Moorthy** is Director, Chennai Chapter of the Observer Research Foundation (ORF), the multi-disciplinary Indian public-policy think-tank, headquartered in New Delhi.

4. **Dr. Vibhuti Singh Shekhawat,** Professor in Humanities and Social Sciences, Malviya National Institute of Technology, Jaipur.

5. **Brigadier Suresh Nair (Retd)** is an independent research scholar on strategic issues.

6. **HuoWenle**, Research Scholar, Jawaharlal Nehru University, New Delhi

7. **Ramnath Reghunadhan** is a Research Scholar at the Department of Humanities and Social Sciences, Indian Institute of Technology Madras, Chennai, India.

8. **Gp Capt A V Chandrasekaran (Retd)** is an Independent Security Analyst.

9. **Aaradhana Singh**, Faculty, Department of Political Science, University of Delhi, Delhi.

10. **Aswani R.S.**, Assistant Professor, Department of Public Policy, University of Petroleum and Energy Studies, Dehradun, Uttarakhand.

11. **Dr P.S. Swathi Lekshmi,** Principal Scientist, Socio-Economic Evaluation and Technology Transfer Division, ICAR-Central Marine

Fisheries Research Institute, Vizhinjam Research Centre, Vizhinjam, Thiruvananthapuram.

12. **Rakhee Viswambharan**, Assistant Professor (on UGC FDP deputation) Department of Political Science, Sree Narayana College, Chempazhanthy (affiliated to University of Kerala) Thiruvananthapuram, Kerala.

Introduction

National security is the prime concern of any nation-state. And there are various means to ensure national security. This includes the traditional means of ensuring national security through military power by one nation or group of nations through military alliances. This system was the only accepted means to meet any threat to security of nations emanates from the military force of other nation or group of nations. However, with the end of cold war and the onset of the non-traditional threat to the security of nations, military power as the only means to address any threat to the security of nation-states has ended. Now no nation-state, whatsoever militarily powerful, can effectively tackle the threat emanates from non-state entities, such as international terrorism. A concerted effort of all nations, small and big militarily powerful and weak is imperative to address the non-traditional threat to national security. Similarly in addressing environmental issues, like climate change, a concerted effort of all nations is required. Thus national security in the 21st century is more complex and demands a multilateral approach.

Maritime security is one of the latest additions to the field of international and national security. The concept has received growing attention especially due to the intensification of concerns over maritime terrorism since 2000. The rise of modern piracy, maritime crimes such as human trafficking, and the increasing importance of the 'blue economy' and issues relating to freedom of navigation, maritime environmental protection and resource management have resulted in the increased significance of maritime security studies. A significant number of states and other international actors have placed maritime security high in their security agenda. This priority is reflected in several governmental and intergovernmental strategies for maritime security. In addition to that, the regional grouping in the Indian Ocean and Indo – Pacific, such as ASEAN, BIMSTEC, IORA, and IONS have placed maritime security issues high in their agenda.

In the modern period especially in the era of globalization oceans have become very important in international trade. Again the potential resource availability from the oceans also enhances its significance. Moreover, the threat to the security of the nation posed by both the state as well as non-state actors can be effectively addressed only through a foolproof security mechanism along the coastal area. Thus the significance of maritime security has enhanced manifold in the 21st century.

In this context, it is very important to look into the latest maritime doctrine brought out by the Indian Navy, which is being mandated to ensure coastal and maritime security of India. The document discusses in detail about the maritime security objectives strategies and measures taken towards the coastal and maritime security of India. The approach of the Indian Navy in ensuring an infallible maritime and coastal security also acknowledged the emergence of a non-traditional threat to the security of India and the role of coastal community in the maritime security matrix.

It appears that coastal security is an important aspect of national security, especially for India with a vast coastline of 7516 kms and also due to the strategic and economic significance of the coastal region. Again the blurred boundary exists between national security and human security emphasis the significance of coastal security. Any investment in terms of coastal area development is an investment not only in human security but also in national security. The infrastructure development along the coastal area also enhances the national security. It is observed that 25 per cent of India's population lives within the 50 kms of the coastal area. In this context the Sagarmala project and coastal area development assumes great significance.

Coastal security being one of the major constituent of maritime security, assumes great significance in the national security of India. However, the multifarious agencies operating at the Union and State/Union Territory level complicate the coordinated planning and implementation of various programme towards coastal security. This has been reflected in the setting up of coastal police also. A uniform pattern of security planning and execution is needed. Under the existing bureaucratic delay and ineffectiveness in planning as well as implementation the task becomes more difficult. Instead of the creation of new institutional mechanism the need for more coordinated activities by the security agencies as well as other agencies such as fishing and port is needed. The information sharing among these agencies is also important. The need for social audit of various coastal security scheme implementations is inevitable to assess the progress achieved in different aspects of coastal security scheme. Similarly, the involvement of coastal community in planning as well as implementation of coastal security schemes is sine quo non for the development of the coastal area and also to assign coastal community the role to act as the 'eyes' and 'ears' of coastal security matrix. All these demand a thorough understanding of the basic features of the coastal terrain and the coastal community.

Recently the V K Krishna Menon Study Centre for International Relations attached to the University of Kerala, Thiruvananthapuram had organized a three day National Seminar on 'Maritime Security of India: Challenges and Policy Options' to address the above stated issues connected with maritime security of India. This volume is a collection of selected papers presented at the national seminar. There are 12 research papers on topic ranging from national security to that of coastal security. In the opening paper Vice Admiral M P Muralidharan, has pointed out the major challenges before maritime security of India His tenure in the Indian Coast Guard as the Director General had marked the implementation of the ambitious Coastal Security Scheme. He has argued that the challenges to National Maritime security could be from threats to economic well-being of the nation ie energy, trade and commerce, living and nonliving resources, or social stability ie crimes in the maritime arena or to political peace ie maritime sovereignty, or even to health of its people ie the environment. He further added that the Geostrategic significance of the seas is well known that 70 per cent of the earth is covered by sea and two third of its population lives within 100 miles of the coast. And 80 per cent of the cities and nearly all major trade and financial centers are along the coast or within 200 km of it. Most major economic and industrial activities also happen within this zone. It is also pertinent that 150 of the 193 member states of United Nations are coastal States. Maritime trade is 80 per cent by volume and 70 per cent by value of the total global trade it involving nearly 53000 ships worth $450 billion generating close to 14 million jobs. As far as India is concerned, he noted that, its strategic perspectives have been influenced by geography, history, culture and geopolitical and economic realities.

Professor Suresh R maintained that Maritime security of India is closely linked to peace and security situation in the Indian Ocean region and India's response towards it. The significance of the Indian Ocean to India's security has long been recognized. However, commensurate with the significance of the Indian Ocean to its national security no major initiative was taken during the cold war period. India's Indian Ocean policy was centered on proposal to the elimination of external power presence from the Indian Ocean through proposals on peace zone in international forums including the UN. Thus India's Indian Ocean policy during this period was solely based on the implementation of UN General Assembly declaration on Indian Ocean as a Zone of Peace (IOZP). A marked change in India's Indian Ocean policy has been reflected in the post-cold war period with the advent of engagement with regional countries and external powers in the Indian Ocean. Similarly, the imperatives of non-traditional threat to its national security also prompted India to collaborate with regional and extra-regional countries in the Indian Ocean region to address the common threat emanates from international terrorism as it demands multilateral approach.

While discussing the apprehensions of small island nations in the Indian Ocean, Sri Lanka and Maldives, Sathiya Moorthy, argues that by their very definition and geography, small island-nations have little or no control over their security. Swayed by the oceans and seas all around, and often with limited resources, including human resources, to man and master the seas from a security perspective, they also suffer from an inherent sense of insecurity *viz* their larger neighbours in particular. Such perceptions, not always justified but not wholly unjustified either, feed constant and continuing anxieties about their sovereignty and territorial integrity.

Dr. Vibhuti Singh Shekhawat argues that Indian maritime security matrix is a complicated web of divergent strands such as British Colonial Legacy modern-day Indian bureaucracy, the clash between generalists and specialists, frequent policy announcements unmatched with suitable, commensurate action, the role of fake strategic think tanks and collusion between multiple security agencies. The irony is that India still does not have an explicitly stated security doctrine which is the major drawback in addressing complex maritime security issues, within the existing system, nothing is hunky-dory and everything appears to be going haywires. While the population is expanding at an enormously fast pace, a large number of fragile eco-systems are getting diluted, disintegrated and ever decimated. Since all systems of mother earth are interconnected and serve as feedback circuits, one finds that marry species are either disappearing or imploding at an incredibly fast rate. He further noted that this creates a dilemma for scientists, experts, policy planners and India's gloated bureaucracy space is getting shortened on the habitable earth. Scientists have formed panels and consultative groups to work out technical back up for study and deliberations.

Brigadier Suresh Nair in his article stated that a look at the map of India here in the context of the Asian Sub Continent gives a fair idea of the immense importance of oceans to it, its positioning in the Asian sub-continent gives it tremendous geographical advantages, clearly underscoring the importance of maritime security to India's wellbeing. But Indian policymakers have been mainly land centric and have harped on the importance of protecting its land borders, of course with sound reasons too. India has the unique distinction of being the only country facing two adversaries both on the Western and Eastern borders. On our Western flank we have a sworn enemy in Pakistan and a powerful rival China along its Northern and Eastern borders. We have a long border with China with whom we had a border war in 1962. Though peace and tranquility by and large prevails, there have been many dangerous military stand offs, the last prominent one being in Doklam on the Sikkim front in 2017. We have fought four wars with Pakistan where the army calls all the shots especially when it comes to defining its relations with India. It has a military doctrine ` to bleed India with thousand cuts' through a set of non-state actors a la terrorists actively fermenting unrest in the Kashmir valley to force its accession to Pakistan. This is enabled through infiltration of terror groups which keeps the Line of Control (LoC) literally on fire. Concurrently, it has also developed close relations with China. It serves the purpose of China to prop up Pakistan, to tie down India's ambitions of being a global player. Thus it is quite justifiable that India's land borders and its defence has been an obsession with Indian policymakers and cannot be neglected. But just as China has understood that the future lies in the Oceans and have made giant strides towards that goal, India too has realized the importance of its vast surrounding oceans and have started emphasizing on the need to enhance its maritime capabilities in the Indian Ocean region and beyond, though may be in a lesser scale than that of China. Maritime security not only involves protection of one's Exclusive Economic Zone (EEZ), but also ensuring freedom of navigation in international waters. It is also just not the physical protection of the seas; it encompasses a vast canvass from protecting the Trade which is linked to the overall economic wellbeing, infrastructure development of ports/harbours, fishing industry, ship building etc., and there are also diplomatic and military aspects to it. He argues that coastal security also assumes huge importance in the light of terrorism especially after 26/11 Mumbai attacks.

A Chinese research scholar, HuoWenle, in his research paper discusses China's maritime security strategy in the Indian Ocean region and claim that it has evolved in three phases: Phase I, from 1949 to mid-

1980s, China could not sustain naval presence in the region due to severe security pressures and limited power projection capabilities; Phase II, from the mid-1980s to 2008, China started and increased its naval presence in the Indian Ocean region; and Phase III, from 2009 to till date, China have achieved permanent presence due to the anti-piracy patrols in the Gulf of Aden and its opening of first overseas military base in Djibouti. Sino-Indian maritime cooperation in the Indian Ocean region includes official visits, ship visits, joint maritime drills and exercises, anti-piracy cooperation, and maritime affairs dialogue, etc. To be sure, Sino-Indian maritime security cooperation is limited now in terms of scope and depth, which reflects the mistrust between China and India. Both China and India are suspicious about each other. China believes that India intends to dominate the Indian Ocean and concerns Indian close maritime security cooperation and coordination with major powers such as United States and Japan, while New Delhi is apprehensive about China's so called 'String of Pearls' strategy, military involvement into the Indian Ocean Region and China's Maritime Silk Road Initiative. Given the mutual nuclear deterrence, economic interdependence and the geopolitical characteristics of the Indian Ocean Region, there is a small chance for China and India to have military conflicts in this region. However, because of the lack of mutual confidence, especially in the strategic and security fields, it is imperative for China and India to further enhance bilateral cooperation on maritime security. He has suggested that such activities include increasing high level official exchanges, warship port visits, joint training and exercises bilaterally and multilaterally, positive cooperation in tackling piracy in the Gulf of Aden, and conducting regular consultations on regional maritime security through effective maritime cooperation dialogues.

Ramnath Reghunadhan maintained that the concept and contextualisation of maritime security is said to have begun in the Pre-historic times by the Egyptians, who is believed to have built the first "war-canoes" in 5500 BCE, on which many art forms in caves and on rocks emerged. It is considered to be one of the earliest instances where recorded the oldest form of naval warfare of the human civilisation is said to have taken place. The conflict over the maritime domain between human would have happened thousands of years preceding that, especially when primitive forms of boats or "rafts" made of "papyrus seeds" have been in use. But, the securitization of maritime domain (at least in modern conception) has only developed with the development and use of war-canoes in and around Northern Africa and later on towards the rest of the world. This also led to the development of ship-building technologies, ancient articulation of maritime operations, and the delineation of maritime domain into "home waters" and/or "foreign waters," along with the origin of maritime forces

Gp Capt A V Chandrasekaran argues that not long ago during the Second World War, airpower earned its spurs and glory over water. The theory of Maritime interdiction—attack of ships— was a major mission for decades in various decisive battles. From Brigadier General William Billy Mitchell's sinking of *Ostfriesland* on 21 July 1921, to the Battle of Midway in 1942, the use of airpower over water made for some dramatic turning points and altered the course of history. "Open and Stable Seas" constitute the basis for peace and prosperity of the international community as a whole. On date the threat of maritime terrorism looms large all around the globe and especially in the turbulent waters of Asia. An act akin to the dramatic attack on 9/11 where in civilian commercial aircraft was used as a cruise missile to perpetuate one of the biggest acts of terror would pale in comparison to acts of maritime terror wherein large luxury cruisers with a huge tourist population can be targeted to inflict mass casualties, or huge oil tankers targeted to choke the vital sea lanes of communications (SLOCs) thereby causing a massive infringement in commercial marine traffic. Both these acts would ensure that the terrorists would get the publicity they hope for thereby motivating more cadres to join the terrorist outfits. The 2008 attacks in Mumbai, India, was another reminder terrorists could exploit relatively open harbours to wreak havoc. To offset these threats the essence of an effective platform which can respond almost immediately, detect, interdict, and effect a decisive counter-attack, with adequate pay load capabilities would be an ideal countermeasure. The element of airpower would be the answer to all maritime terrorism woes as it possesses all the above mentioned capabilities and more in abundance. In the words of former secretary of state Hilary Clinton "We may be dealing with a 17th century crime, but we need to bring 21st century solutions to bear." The air power has an array of unmanned aerial vehicles, both armed and unarmed, helicopters and amphibious planes to be extremely persistent and be precise in its targeting. Clear perspectives on the nature and likelihood of specific types of maritime terrorist attacks are essential for prioritizing the nation's maritime anti-terrorism activities. In practice, however, there has been considerable public debate about the likelihood of scenarios frequently given high priority by federal policy makers, such as nuclear or "dirty" bombs smuggled in shipping containers, liquefied natural gas (LNG) tanker attacks, and attacks on passenger ferries. Differing priorities set by port officials, grant officials, and legislators lead to differing allocations of port security resources and levels of protection against specific types of attacks. How they ultimately relate to one another under a national maritime security strategy remains to be seen. He further argued that the maritime terrorist threats to India are varied, and so are the nation's efforts to combat them.

Aaradhana Singh in her research paper maintained that India has emerged as an important Asian power with the advent of 21st century. At the global level also, it has become an important player and sharing all important global and Asian multilateral platforms. Since the end of cold war, the locus of global system has started to tilt towards Asia and according to global economic pundits, Asia will be representing more than half of the global GDP. It has further changed the dynamics of bilateral and multilateral relations in Asia. We are aware of the fact that a wide array of opinions was expressed since the end of the cold war on the idea that Asia will be an important player in the coming decades. At the end of the cold war, debates started on new lines by the formulators of foreign policy that both World system and Asian system must be multi-polar. This is one of the most significant issue where India and China diverge as China's underlying problem lies. China does not have a problem with world being multi-polar but it wants Asian balance of power to be unipolar super headed by China. Japan also thinks similar to Indian line and thus the bilateral relationship between India and Japan has been deepening since the end of the cold war. India-Japan relationship has grown rapidly since last one decade. Due to inherent geopolitical, economic and strategic dimensions, this bilateral relationship is all set to reformulate new Asian balance of power based on multiplicity. China, Japan, India and Vietnam are indulged in reformulating the balance of power within Asia. Other Asian countries also do not China's supremacy and thus their bonhomie with the competitors of China is deepening in an excellent manner since last one decade and all set to grow in the foreseeable future. In recent years, China has exposed its intention to use force to capture Islands under Japanese rule since many decades. In various regions of China, protests had been organized against Japan including Hong Kong protests, which demanded capture of Japan ruled Islands in the East China Sea. Including United States, India had also insisted amicable resolution of disputes and adherence to international law by all concerned parties. Due to border disputes with China, India has also been apprehensive about Chinese steps and that also has strengthened its bilateral relationship with Japan in a massive manner. These events vindicate that balance of power theory is working well in Asian theater and all set to sustain the process due to Chinese reluctance to accommodate the aspirations of other countries. She had further argued that the new balance of power in Asia is all set to reshape existing power architecture.

In her research article Aswani R S, opined that International relations is mostly deliberated as a conflict-based paradigm in which the main actors are nation-states for whom power and security become the central issues, and in which there is hardly any value for morality. Fear and lack of trust become the basis of all actions and it contributes to an underlying presence of security dilemma in all the activities of nation states. Indian Ocean Region (IOR) also projects a security dilemma that has created complex political relations. The Indian Ocean Region has turned into a center of global power conflicts in the 21st century mainly due to the impending war between India and China for dominance in these warm waters and due to the fluid political scenario in the Middle East and the surging value of Persian oil in the global market. Bouchard & Crumplin (2010), added to these variants the renewed interests of a new triangular play, 'American's heavy military interventionism, China's arrival on the regional chessboard and the rise of India as a real Indian Ocean great power.' She maintain that 21st century has seen a strategic reassessment of the global geopolitical significance of IOR

The scientist from CMFRI, Swathi Lekshmi pointed out that India has nine coastal States and four Union Territories. It is blessed with a long coast line of 7,517 Km, of which 5,422 kms lie in the mainland and the rest is distributed on the islands in the nine States and four Union Territories. The coastal Union Territories which are island areas being Andaman and Nicobar and the Lakshadweep islands, the former with a coastline of 132 km and the latter with a coastline of 1,962 km. The highly indented coastline of the country makes it vulnerable to security threats and infiltration by terrorist and militant attack in addition to other threats such as smuggling and carrying of arms and ammunition. A per estimates 95 percent of India's trade by volume and 70 percent by value is done through maritime transport. This assumes strategic importance more so because India sits centrally at the cross roads of Trans Indian Ocean Routes. The cargo ships sailing between East Asia, America, Europe and Africa pass through Indian Territorial waters. Added to this, there has been an unsettled and disputed nature of some of India's maritime boundaries. India shares 14,880 km of boundary with Pakistan, China, Nepal, Bhutan, Myanmar and Bangladesh (Das, 2010). Including a small segment with Afghanistan (106 km) in northern Jammu and Kashmir (J&K), now part of the Northern Areas of Pakistan Occupied Kashmir (POK), India's land borders exceed 15,000 km shared with seven countries. The coastline of peninsular India is bordered by the Bay of Bengal in the east, the Indian Ocean in the south and the Arabian sea in the west. India shares its maritime boundaries with seven countries namely, Pakistan, the Maldives, Sri Lanka, Indonesia, Thailand, Myanmar and Bangladesh

Rakhee Viswambharan in her research paper has claimed that in the post-cold war period the threat to the security of nation states emanates mainly from non-state actors. Unlike the attack from state actors the non-state actors mode of attack is different. It demands a constant vigil throughout the land and maritime borders. Coastal security is one of the subsets of maritime security. The coastal security has become an urgent necessity especially in the context of the 2008 Mumbai terrorist attack and the threat it poses to the national security. The 2012 Italian marine issue have added a new dimension to the security of the coastal people engaged in fishing. When we look into the coastal security a convergence of the national security concerns and human security concerns is visible. The overall development of the coastal area would lead to better human security and better human security would result in enlisting the support of the coastal community to ensure national security programme, especially the coastal security. However the task of guarding the vast coastline, unlike our land borders, is a complex issue involving multiple stake holders such as shipping, fisheries, offshore exploration and production, tourism, and scientific community. In short, she has maintained that coastal security is not only about protecting our coastal terrain and territorial waters from direct attacks from state actors or non-state actors, but also safeguarding the interests of all stakeholders.

The above twelve papers discuss in detail various dimensions of maritime security of India. The contributors include leading academics, research scholars, defence experts and practitioners. We hope that this would further encourage deliberations and consequent action in strengthening maritime security of India, which assumes great significance in the national security matrix. It is noted that policy formation is as important as its effective implementation in a time bound manner. There is no dearth of policy in the maritime security domain, however, when it comes to implementation there is bureaucratic delay, and many programme still remain in paper. The need for effective evaluation of the policy implementation by an external agency other than bureaucracy is imperative. Similarly it is also important to monitor the effective use of scarce resources. It appears that coastal police in many states and union territories are still at the budding stage and the weakest link in the maritime security programme. The coastal police personnel also lack necessary training and expertise to use the machines and equipment delivered to them as part of the ambitious Coastal Security Scheme I & II. It is also important to equip and empower the coastal community to perform the role as the 'eyes' and 'ears' of coastal security matrix.

Maritime security of India is closely linked to peace and security situation in the Indian Ocean region and India's response towards it. The significance of the Indian Ocean to India's security has long been recognized. The recent shift in India's Indian Ocean policy from elimination of external powers to engagement with external powers is in tune with changing dimensions of security threat to national security. The imperatives of non-traditional threat to national security also have prompted India to collaborate with regional and extra regional countries in the Indian Ocean region to address the common threat emanates from international terrorism as it demand multilateral approach. Again, in the era of accelerated pace of globalization and subsequent increase in international trade, it is imperative to protect the sea lanes of trade and communication free from any interruption. It is imperative that policymakers and think tanks should come out of the cold war theories of power rivalry and significance of choke points and focus their attention more on human security concerns. In short, maritime security assumes great significance not only in terms of ensuring national security ingrained in human security but also the protection of global commons through joint endeavour.

–Dr SURESH R.

Maritime Security of India: Challenges and Policy Options

Vice Admiral M P Muralidharan AVSM, NM

Maritime security in the 21st century assumes a much broader definition than the often perceived military one. Challenges to National Maritime security could be from threats to the economic well-being of the national energy, trade and commerce, living and nonliving resources, or social stability i.e., crimes in the maritime arena or to political peace i.e., maritime sovereignty, or even to the health of its people i.e., the environment.

As far as India is concerned, our quintessential maritime character and geostrategic location are factors that have defined our growth as a nation over the centuries. Needless to say, India's national security has been closely linked with the oceans. Sardar KM Panicker, one of our more perceptive historians, had foreseen importance of affairs Maritime in the nation's destiny. He had said "India had never lost her independence till she lost command of the sea." He had further concluded that "India's security lies on the Indian Ocean. Without a well-considered and effective naval policy, India's position will be weak, dependent on others and her freedom at the mercy of any country capable of controlling the Indian Ocean." In my view, his words are even more relevant today, with the growing importance of seas for trade and commerce and our economic growth. I would only add that today we need to look beyond the Indian Ocean and consider Indo-Pacific region, more so as the world itself shifted focus from the 20th century Euro - Atlantic view, to an Indo-Pacific one, making this region critically important to all major powers.

The end of the cold war era towards the close of the 20th century, also witnessed a shift from traditional Naval confrontation on the high seas, to challenges both conventional and non-conventional in the littoral region. Littoral security, therefore, emerged as a vital dimension of maritime security. As a result India too had to review her security and threat perceptions in the maritime area. In addition to persistent threats and challenges of traditional nature, the maritime security environment around India has become even more complex and unpredictable, due to the expansion in the scale of a variety of non- traditional threats. This audience is well aware of the terrorist attacks of 26/11 in Mumbai, which demanded a complete re-evaluation of India's security organisation and operating philosophy.

The Geostrategic significance of the seas is well known that 70 per cent of the earth is covered by the sea and two third of its population lives within 100 nautical miles of the coast. And 80 per cent of the cities and nearly all major trade and financial centers are along the coast or within 200 km of it. Most major economic and industrial activities also happen within this zone. It is also pertinent that 150 of the 193 member states of United Nations are coastal States. Maritime trade is 80 per cent by volume and 70 per cent by value of the total global trade it involving nearly 53000 ships worth $450 billion generating close to 14 million jobs.

As far as India is concerned, her strategic perspectives have been influenced by geography, history, culture and geopolitical and economic realities. It is particularly relevant that India is both a Continental and as well as a Maritime nation, with a territory of over 3 million square km, with a land frontier of 15,000 km. India's coastline, on the other hand, is over 7500 km, with nine Coastal States, four Union territories and close to 1200 Islands, with an Exclusive Economic Zone of 2.2 million square km with another 0.5 million sq. km to be added in the continental shelf. Its location at the base of continental Asia, on top of the Indian Ocean close to the choke points of the ocean, gives it a vantage position in relation to the entire area from the African coast and West Asia, to South East Asia and beyond into the Pacific Ocean. It gives India an added stake in the security and stability of waters in the Indo-Pacific region more so as it is located close to the largest source of oil and natural gas in the world, i.e., the Gulf Nations as well as Central Asia. 50% of the world's Maritime trade flows through the Indian Ocean, which includes nearly 50% of the container traffic and almost 70% of the global trade in oil and natural gas.

Let us now briefly touch upon the conventional military Maritime challenges. Pakistan continues to encourage terrorist elements that are inimical to India and this remains the greatest single threat to peace and stability in this region. It is also worth remembering that critical energy needs of India flow from the Persian Gulf and the normal traffic lanes passes close to Pakistan. It is therefore susceptible to interdiction in times of conflict. Not to mention unconventional threats posed by terrorist elements nurtured by Pakistan. While in any conventional conflict, Pakistani Maritime forces would need to be comprehensively marginalised, regular patrolling and monitoring of the sea lanes through which Indian cargo moves is a major peace time Maritime challenge. As regards China, while we have a scholar speaking in the seminar on this issue, it is evident that China has her economic interests at stake in the Indian Ocean region. Therefore she has been actively engaging India's neighbors by developing their Maritime and military infrastructure and also extending economic help. The so called string of pearls strategy of bases and diplomatic ties from Africa to Middle East and South Asia are all a vital part of this strategy. While I do not foresee in the immediate future, any repeat of a 1962 type of conflict, as it would harm economic progress of both the Nations, we have witnessed confrontation along the land borders. While they were resolved by discussions and dialogue, it is evident that unless India is able to argue from a position of strength, its views would be hardly relevant. I would like to state that while we need to positively engage with China as well as Pakistan to avoid any direct confrontation, we should also develop our Land and Maritime forces to prevent any adventurism in our littoral by any power. While it is not necessary to specify in the bean count methodology the kind of force levels that we may need in the maritime arena, it would suffice to say that we need combat ready forces which are capable of countering any threats in the littoral area, as well as forces which by their very presence in areas outside our immediate neighborhood, can deter development of threats.

Let us now move on to non-conventional Maritime security challenges which are also called LIMO or Low Intensity Maritime Operations and would include maritime terrorism, piracy, drug and human trafficking, gun-running, poaching or IUU and could also include an illegal gathering of sensitive seismic and economic data. In this regard, a major problem that India faces is that many of the islands in our Island territories, both in the Andaman and Nicobar as well as in Lakshadweep, are uninhabited and are therefore susceptible to use as hideouts or havens for trans-shipment or caching of arms or drugs or other illegal activities. It is also pertinent that there are merchantmen of various types engaged in dubious maritime trade, registered under Flags of Convenience which are difficult to track, as they routinely change names and registry.

Even though there have been a number of terrorist attacks on ships including the more famous Cole and Limburg cases, and closer home the sea tigers of LTTE, historically, the world's oceans have not been a major focus for terrorist activity. It is estimated that maritime terror incidents constitute only about 2% of all international terror attacks in the last three decades. While terror organisations aspire to operate with impunity in the world's waterways and seas, the lone disincentive is the complexities associated with the marine environment. Operating at sea requires mariner skills, access to appropriate assault and transport vehicles, the ability to mount and sustain operations from a non-land based environment; all specialist capabilities, that are not easy to acquire. Ominously, the attack by terrorists at Mumbai on the night of 26 Nov 2008 saw professional exploitation of the maritime environment and therefore maritime terrorist activity remains a major challenge. Drug trafficking and gun running are often taken as adjuncts to terrorism. Drug trafficking is considered a lucrative way to finance terrorism. Indian coastline with innumerable landing places is susceptible to both these activities as observed post the blasts in Mumbai. However regular patrolling has now reduced these threats, but they still exist. Piracy is another major challenge that emerged just when it was thought that piracy was only in Hollywood! But combined patrolling and regular exchange of intelligence and cooperative efforts such as RECAPP have reduced the threat of piracy to an extent. While Indian security forces have been part of combined efforts to tackle piracy, we have had no major impact of this menace in our waters. Human trafficking or illegal immigration is another security challenge. While we have had such immigration in the Andaman's area, recently there were reports of attempts from Kerala coast! This, however, is not a major threat as of now in our waters.

Moving onto economic and technological challenges, maintenance of smooth flow of trade and energy supplies holds the key to economic well-being of any state. Since 80% of the world's trade by volume, which in our case is 90%, is transported over the oceans, the security of sea lanes of communications is a major challenge that needs to be ensured at all times. While in times of conflict a host of military and procedural measures would be put into place to ensure safety of trade and energy supplies, it needs to be ensured even in peacetime. In my view, India has a stake and regional responsibility in ensuring that the sea lanes of communications in the Indian Ocean remain open at all times and there is no disruption of maritime traffic especially at choke points. This is more so in view of globalised nature of world trade and economy. May I also add that a major part of Indian trade is in foreign flagged vessels. Hence the security of shipping, ports and connected infrastructure remains a major challenge.

Energy security encompasses not only safety of sea lanes of communications or protection of ships carrying oil and gas, but would include defense of our coastal and offshore energy infrastructure, such as refineries, offshore platforms, pipelines single boy moorings. India also has a stake in security of her overseas exploration efforts. With hydrocarbon interests becoming transnational and extending worldwide, with pipelines running across National boundaries, future threats would include disruption of such energy flows and would therefore pose a major challenge to maritime security forces.

No discussion on Maritime security challenges would be complete without mention of the 2.2 million square km of EEZ of our nation, which as indicated would increase with continental shelf delineation. We have a Pioneer investor status with 1.5 lakh square km in Central Indian Ocean, for recovery and processing of polymetallic nodules. While technology today does not make it commercially viable to extract such nodules, with progress of technology we would undertake such activities. There would be a need to ensure safety and security of such activities. We also have interests in Antarctica, where possibly in not too distant future there would be prospects of resource exploitation. While we develop economically viable technologies singly or together with like-minded nations, to harness the ocean wealth, we need to prevent unauthorised exploitation of resources and this would also include preventing surreptitious gathering of seismic data in our exclusive economic zone. Safeguarding of our ocean assets is, therefore, a major challenge.

Illegal, Unreported and Unregulated (IUU) fishing constitutes one of the most common and widespread maritime security challenges. It is also one of the most economically damaging. Essentially it is illegal fishing conducted in waters under the jurisdiction of a state, without its permission, or in contravention of its laws and regulations. Globally, IUU fishing is estimated to be between 20 and 25 million tons of fish annually i.e. about 20 to 30% of total fisheries production. It is estimated that annual losses due to illegal fishing is between $ 10 to 23 bn. Fishing is a major economic activity in India with 2.5 lakh fishing vessels, generating employment for 15 million people and fetching an income of $6 bn. Hence any IUU in our waters directly affects our economy.

Environmental security is another issue that needs to be looked at with over 60 thousand ships transiting the Indian Ocean. Major oil spills are a realistic possibility as there could be collisions, groundings, or even damage to ships due to terrorist attacks. Spill from offshore platform accidents are also a distinct possibility. There have also been instances of dumping of toxic waste by passing ships and discharge of toxic material from ships that come to ship breaking yards. Any major oil or other chemical spills close to our shores would be disastrous to the environment and to the livelihood of those who depend on the coastal zone for their sustenance. Enhanced patrolling and closer monitoring is essential to prevent such threats.

While it cannot be strictly termed as a security challenge, search and rescue and disaster relief, or HADR ie humanitarian assistance and disaster and disaster relief as we now call it is another major challenge to security forces at sea. Prediction mechanisms, warning systems, contingency plans and rapid reaction forces need to be put in place to mitigate the effects of disasters like Tsunami or cyclones when they happen. Smaller nations in the Indian Ocean region do lookup to Nations like India for help and evacuation assistance. Evacuation of the Indian diaspora by maritime forces is another challenge.

The key to Maritime security is increasing awareness of activities in the maritime domain in other words Maritime domain awareness or MDA as it is termed. Collection, analysis, fusion and timely dissemination of enormous quantities of data from diverse agencies ranging from space based surveillance, aerial recce, automatic tracking and so on would be the key to ensuring maritime security and meeting challenges that they pose.

It would be clearly evident that maritime security and the challenges it poses has become vastly complex and demand innovative approaches. I would also say that current threats to maritime security do not recognise political boundaries and there is obviously limit to what an individual state can do to counter maritime threats. Globalized economy has further enhanced the interdependence of nations. Oceans have often been referred to as common heritage of mankind and therefore cooperation between all stake holders is necessary to safeguard common maritime interests. Trust and confidence between nations is essential to ensure cooperative security. Confidence building could begin in the form of bilateral and multilateral dialogues and conferences which could be followed up with exercises between Maritime Forces of nations. High level contacts and regular meetings among political and military leaders of countries could further institutionalize the process and sustain continuity.

India's geographic position enables it to strategically influence not only its own economic growth but also those of many other nations in the Indo-Pacific region. India's maritime strategy, therefore, should be one encompassing all maritime activities to safeguard her military, economic, commercial, scientific and political interests. Her maritime forces, the Navy and the Coast Guard, therefore, need to be developed to support such a strategy. Even though the need of the hour is cooperative security, unless one has sufficient force levels and economic strength, one may be compelled to compromise national interests.

International cooperation with transverse trans-regional linkages in intelligence, surveillance, network and data sharing backed by a robust and effective system of patrolling would allow Nations and Maritime agencies to monitor the oceans more effectively. It would be recalled that many years ago, the then CNO of USN Admiral Michael G Mullen, had advocated a Thousand Ship Navy, a phrase that denoted cooperative of Navies to police the oceans.

India has over the years been leveraging international cooperation in the maritime area by participating and conducting bilateral and multilateral dialogues and symposiums. The Indian Navy and Indian Coast Guard have also been regularly exercising with maritime forces of other nations to enhance inter-operability and confidence building. Prime Minister Dr. Manmohan Singh, while commissioning the Indian Naval Academy in January 2009, summed the issue by saying that "Naval power is not just about warfighting but also about diplomacy, commerce and energy security among other things."

From an Indian perspective it is obvious that maritime security challenges must be addressed on a multi-layered basis. While those predominantly located around the Indian coast could be tackled by our forces by regular surveillance and patrolling, many other challenges would require bilateral or even multilateral approach. This would be more so in resolving transnational crimes and maintaining Maritime order.

The seamless nature of maritime domain enables a steady flow of threats and challenges from one area to another. In order to safeguard its maritime interests, India would need to endeavor to build favourable and positive maritime environment and enhance net Maritime Security all along the Indian Ocean region in cooperation with Maritime Forces from friendly nations. While substantial steps have been taken since the 26/11 attacks on Mumbai, we cannot afford to rest on our oars. These measures would need to be strengthened so as to prevent, repulse and eliminate threats to India's security in coastal and offshore areas. A collaborative and coordinated approach by the Indian Maritime forces ie the Navy, the Coast Guard, the Coastal Police and other stakeholders including the coastal community is, therefore, the need of the hour to face such challenges.

To conclude, by quoting our first Prime Minister Pandit Jawaharlal Nehru, who aptly summed up importance of Maritime Security in India's prosperity. He said "And from this ship, I looked at India and thought of the county and its geographical situation. On three sides of it there is sea and on the fourth high mountains. In a sense, our country may be set to be in the very lap of the oceans. In these circumstances, I pondered over our close links with the sea and how the sea has brought us together. From time immemorial people of India had very intimate connections with the sea. They had trade with other countries and had also built ships. Later the country became weak. ----- Now that we are free, we have once again realized the importance of the sea. We cannot afford to be weak at sea."

Maritime Security and India's Indian Ocean Policy: From External Powers Elimination to Engagement

Dr Suresh R.

Maritime security of India is closely linked to peace and security situation in the Indian Ocean region and India's response towards it. The significance of the Indian Ocean to India's security has long been recognized. However, commensurate with the significance of the Indian Ocean to its national security no major initiative was taken during the cold war period. India's Indian Ocean policy was centered on proposal to the elimination of external power presence from the Indian Ocean through proposals on peace zone in international forums including the UN. Thus India's Indian Ocean policy during this period was solely based on the implementation of UN General Assembly declaration on Indian Ocean as a Zone of Peace (IOZP). A marked change in India's Indian Ocean policy has been reflected in the post-cold war period with the advent of engagement with regional countries and external powers in the Indian Ocean. Similarly, the imperatives of non-traditional threat to its national security also prompted India to collaborate with regional and extra regional countries in the Indian Ocean region to address the common threat emanates from international terrorism as it demand multilateral approach.

Indian Ocean - Geopolitical and Strategic Importance

The Indian Ocean, which is the third largest Ocean in the world, is surrounded by Asia, Africa, Antarctica and Australia; the northern limits of the Indian Ocean are well defined by the landmass. The dividing line between the Atlantic and the Indian Ocean is the meridian of Cape Agulhas (20 deg.0 min.E). The meridian of the South-East Cape of Tasmania (147 deg.0 min.E), the western exit of the Bass Strait and the median line between North-West Australia and the Peninsula of Malay (the Cape of Talbot through Timor, Sumba, Flores and Sunda Island up to Sumatra) from the dividing line between the Pacific Ocean and the Indian Ocean. The dividing line between the Antartic Ocean and the Indian Ocean is the 60 deg. 0 min. South latitude[1]. The total area of the Indian Ocean is 74.92 million square kilometers[2], which is 20.7 percent of the world's sea area and 14 percent of the earth's surface[3]. The average depth of the Indian Ocean is 38.59 kilometres[4]. The main constituent parts of the Indian Ocean are the Red Sea, the Arabian Sea, the Bay of Bengal, the Andaman Sea, the Persian Gulf, the Mosambique Channel and the Great Australian Bight. The Indian Ocean differs from the Pacific and the Atlantic Ocean in two important aspects. First, it is land-locked in the north, does not extend into the cold climatic region of the Northern Hemisphere and consequently is asymmetrical with regard to its circulation. Second, the wind system over its equatorial and northern portion changes twice each year causing an almost complete reversal of its circulation.[5] Of all the oceans, the Indian Ocean offers the most suitable navigational environment round the year. Its winds are often predictable and remain at below gale force. It is mostly free from fog, mist and treacherous currents.

Geopolitics

Five narrow stretches of water, the Bab-el-Mandeb, the Strait of Hormuz, the Strait of Malacca, the Cape of Good Hope and the Sundra Strait, guard the eastern and western entrance to the Indian Ocean.[6] The Bab-el-Mandeb is the southern tip of the Suez Canal; the strait of Hormuz stands sentinel over the oil flow by sea from Persian Gulf; the strait of Malacca and the Sundra Strait control the seaborne traffic from the western Pacific Ocean; and the Cape of Good Hope overlooks the shipping route around Africa[7]. From Pacific Ocean the Indian Ocean can be approached through Torrs Strait, the Arafura Sea, Timor Sea, Lombak, Sunda Straits, Malacca Strait, Bass Strait and even from the South of Australia. It is approachable from the Atlantic Ocean either through the Cape of Good Hope route or through the Gibralter straits, Mediterranean sea, the Suez Canal, the Red Sea and then through the Strait of Bab-el-Mandeb. The major sea routes, from Europe to East Asia, the Indian sub-continent, Australia and from the USA to the Indian sub-continent pass through the Indian Ocean. The minor sea routes are from Europe to West Asia, the East Africa and Mauritius[8]

Indian Ocean Choke Points

Nine important passages provide access into the Indian Ocean, of which five are key energy Seas Lines of Communications (SLOC). Choking any one of them would cause disruption of seaborne trade, and uncontrolled volatility in oil and commodity prices, leading to upheavals in the global economy.

The major choke points[9] are:

1. Strait of Hormuz

2. Suez Canal

3. Strait of Bab-el-Mandeb

4. Malacca Strait

5. Lombok Strait

6. Sunda Strait

7. Six Degree Channel

8. Nine Degree Channel

9. Cape of Good Hope

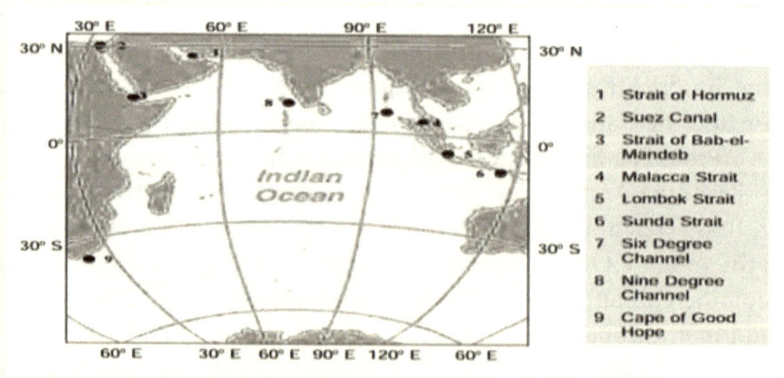

Choke Points in IOR

Map 1 Choke Points in the Indian Ocean Region

The Strait of Hormuz. Hormuz is the world's most strategic choke point. Connecting the Arabian Sea to the Gulf of Oman and the Persian Gulf, it has channels 2 nautical miles (nm) wide for both inward and outbound traffic with a Pipeline, forcing them to round the southern tip of Africa instead. This would add greatly to transit time and cost, and effectively tie-up spare tanker capacity.

The Malacca Strait. The Strait of Malacca links the Indian Ocean with the Pacific Ocean. Being on the shortest sea route connecting the Persian Gulf with East Asia and USA, it is a critical chokepoint in the IOR. At its narrowest point, in the Philip Channel, the Malacca Strait is only 1.5 nm wide. This creates a natural bottleneck, with potential for blockage in case of collision or grounding of ships. Closure of the strait would entail re-routing of nearly half the world's fleet, generating a requirement for additional vessel capacity and resulting in immediate increase in worldwide freight costs.

The Suez Canal and extra-regional Red Sea. The Suez Canal is the gateway between Europe and Asia. It is 105.4 nm long and, being entirely at sea level, does not require any locks for its operation. Closure of the Suez Canal would cause traffic to be diverted around the Cape of Good Hope, thereby increasing the transit time and transportation costs.

The Strait of Bab-el-Mandeb and Horn of Africa. The Bab-el-Mandeb connects the Gulf of Aden and the Red Sea. Closure of the Bab-el- Mandeb would keep tankers loaded in the Persian Gulf from reaching the Suez Canal or the Sumed.

The Lombok Strait. At a minimum channel width of 11.5 nm, the Lombok Strait has sufficient width and depth and is far less congested than the Malacca Strait. Ships too large for the Strait of Malacca use this passage.

The Sunda Strait. An alternate route to the Malacca and Lombok Straits is the Sunda Strait, which is 50 nm long and 15 nm wide at its northeast entrance. Large ships avoid passage through this strait due to depth restrictions and strong currents.

The Six Degree Channel. The primary passage through the Andaman and Nicobar Islands to the Strait of Malacca is through the Six Degree Channel or Great Channel. Stretching from Indira Point on Great Nicobar to the northern tip of Aceh on the Indonesian island of Sumatra, it is an easy and wide passage without any depth limitations.

The Nine Degree Channel. The Nine Degree Channel is the most direct route through India's Lakshadweep Islands for ships sailing from the Persian Gulf bound for East Asia.

The Cape of Good Hope. The Cape of Good Hope is not a conventional choke point since adequate depth of water lies to its south and the passage of ships is not restricted by land. However, economic sense and unfavorable currents demand that ships pass close to land, which makes them susceptible to attack and grounding.

Indian Ocean - Strategic Importance

The strategic importance of the Indian Ocean lies in its geographic setting as it is a sea-line of communication between the East and West. Further since power can exercise by controlling islandic territories of the Indian Ocean they are strategically important. These include from the west to eastward, Mallagasy, Comoros, Seychelles, Chogos Archipelago, Socotra, Indian Coral Atoll, Laccadives, Sri Lanka, the chain of 219 islandic spots of Andaman and Nicobar stretching from South-western tip of Myanmar to the northern end of Sumatra, Mrgui Archipelago and the Cocao islands. These islands have served as the maritime station from the very beginning and were colonized in the 17th and 18th centuries to act as stepping stones to the 'Eastern treasures'. Besides the islands, the Indian Ocean cuts across the mainland at various places, thus forming a large number of gulfs, like the Persian Gulf, Gulf of Oman, Aden, Aquba, Suez and Cambay which are also strategically significant.

Geopolitical importance of Indian Ocean Region

The Indian Ocean region includes 36 littoral and 11 hinterland[10] states making a total of 47 independent states with 30 per cent of the world population. The vast majority of the Indian Ocean littoral and hinterland countries attained their independence from the European colonial powers only after the end of the Second World War. Most of these countries in the region were either colonies, trust territories or protectorates under the British Empire which controlled the political, military and economic activities of the region till recent times. The economy of the regional countries were almost ruined by the colonialism and artificial national boundaries were drawn without any geographic, linguistic or ethnic considerations leading to intra-regional conflicts once the colonial powers left the Indian Ocean region. Moreover, in the western countries, economic and industrial revolution took place first which was followed by social and

Map 2- Indian Ocean Region

political revolution, whereas in the Indian Ocean regional countries the political revolution preceded the economic and industrial revolutions. This led to social and political tensions in these countries. Politically, the region has a strange admixture of democracy, military dictatorship, totalitarianism, absolute monarchy and constitutional monarchy; several regimes in the region are politically unstable and provide a fertile ground for external intervention. In 1960's the commercial activities in the region increased enormously and the presence of natural resources of oil made the great powers have shown much interest in the region. All the countries in the region, except Australia, South Africa and Israel are developing countries. The above-mentioned three countries and Thailand are not members of the Non-aligned Movement (NAM).[11] It is the memories of colonialism, the desire to avoid entanglement in great power rivalries and the need to devote their resources to development that have led the vast majority of the countries in the Indian Ocean region to adopt the Non-aligned policy.[12]

Economically, the region has a great many diversities and disparities. The African region with its 8.7 million square km is marked with uneven and underdeveloped resources and low technological development low standard of living with very high annual growth rate of population. The Asian region with its 12.5 million square km of area has an uneven distribution of population, high pressure of population on its resource base, high growth rate of population, underdevelopment nature of economy, low standard of living and low technology development. The Australian region is fairly developed like the South African area. The economy in the Indian Ocean region is predominantly agricultural in nature and the industrial base is weak.

Considering the population, the food production is less than the requirement, which put definite limitation on the countries in the region. The region is estimated to include more than 60 per cent of the world crude oil reserves[13] and is an important source of raw material and strategic minerals such as chromium, bauxite, uranium and manganese. Most of these materials are exported to the industrialized countries. The local economics lack the infrastructure necessary for the processing and full industrial exploitation of these materials. The relative dependence of these countries on the great powers for capital, technological know-how and technology transfer and manufactured goods is a very important factor influencing their external behavior. The vast mineral resources and commercial crops added to the Indian Ocean region's strategic importance in relation to the industrially advanced countries in Europe, USA, Japan, China and Russia.

The surveys conducted in the Indian Ocean sea-bed reveals rich stocks of nodules of manganese, nickel, cobalt, copper, molybdenum etc. Calculations show that one square mile of the sea-bed, where nodules are located could produce about 70,000 tons of minerals which would yield in value about $ 4, 00,000. One square mile of such nodules will yield among other mineral 30,000 tons of Iron ore, 3,600 tons of aluminum 2,300 tons of manganese, 400 tons of cobalt, 1,200 tons of nickel and 650 tons of copper.[14] The Indian Ocean has got extensive marine food potentiality. The estimates show that the sea-bed can provide more than 12 million tons of catch fish every year. Again one fifth of the world's total arable land lies in this region producing crops like wheat, rice, tea, coffee and cotton. In the Indian Ocean littoral and hinterland countries huge deposits of gold and diamonds are concentrated.[15]

The Indian Ocean carries a substantial proportion of international trade,[16] even though the industrial production in the Indian Ocean region is less in relation to the world production. The natural resources of the region greatly contribute to this factor. Approximately one-fourth of the entire cargo carried in world marine trade and about two-third of oil are loaded or unloaded in the ports of the Indian Ocean region. Most of the countries in the Indian Ocean were colonies till 1945 and are not as developed as the countries in the west. The region could not play an effective role in world affairs because of it's under developed economies.

Again, unlike the developed world, the Indian Ocean region abounds with conflict situations and bilateral and multilateral negotiation as a means to settle disputes peacefully has been very rarely employed. This has provided ample opportunities for external powers to the Indian Ocean to interfere in the affairs of the countries in the Indian Ocean region.

India's Indian Ocean Policy

In 1947, when India became independent the cold war had already started and the world was divided into two antagonistic blocs, one led by the USA and the other by former USSR. India decided not to join any of the blocs but to pursue an independent foreign policy[17]. India played a major role in the Bandung Conference of Afro-Asian nations held in April 1955 which laid the foundation of the Non-aligned Movement. India was one of the founder members of the Non-aligned Movement.

In the immediate post-independence period India's interests in the Indian Ocean were largely commercial and defensive. Its economic interests in the Indian Ocean were few; largely due to inadequate technological capabilities it did not investigate and exploit its oceanic resources, with the exception of fisheries. India's commercial interest stemmed from its dependence on the Indian Ocean sea lanes for sea borne trade. India's security interests and requirement centered mainly around its land frontiers particularly Pakistan in the North-West.

A study group of the Indian Council of World Affairs in 1957 stated rightly the importance of Indian Ocean to India:

To India, the security of this region is of paramount importance as oceanic routes across this ocean carry the bulk of her overseas trade. If these routes come under the control of countries not friendly to India, this would threaten very seriously her economic and industrial development, in fact, her very independence. Three sides of India's frontier are bordered by water-a serious matter. This cannot be lightly dismissed... India although committed to a policy of non-alignment cannot possibly neglect her seaward defences. She has unquestionably got to think of having adequate naval forces to protect the miles and miles of her coastline ....[18]

Even though the importance of the Indian Ocean to India's security was repeatedly[19] stressed India was constrained to give less attention to the navy than land forces. This was due to a number of factors; first, the threat posed by Pakistan in the North West, second the threat posed by China in the North, third, the fact that Britain was a dominant power in the Indian Ocean which provided India some comfort because its presence was without any adverse spin off and fourth, in the overall planning of immediate dangers the threat from the Indian Ocean appeared least alarming and hence the continued neglect of the Indian Ocean as a security threat.

The then Prime Minister of India, Jawaharlal Nehru commenting upon the entry of the US Seventh Fleet into the Indian Ocean, said on 19 December 1963; "If anything is obviously to our detriment we protest if not we do not". He also stated; "The Indian Ocean is a vast area, we cannot say anybody cannot go round the area."[20] India took such a stand because at that time India favored the US presence as a counter measure to the threat posed by China.[21] This stand of India had undergone a minor change in mid-1960's and India expressed mild protest[22] on the British decision to develop defense facilities in British Indian Ocean Territory along with the US in the Indian Ocean. But by the late sixties India strongly opposed the outside great power presence in the Indian Ocean.[23] Towards the end of 1969 India had also decided to increase its naval capability and sought the cooperation of the countries in the Indian Ocean region to take steps for making Indian Ocean an area of peace and opposed the induction of outside forces into the Indian Ocean.[24]

Peace and Security Efforts in the Indian Ocean during the Cold War Period

In the early 1970's most of the Non-aligned countries of the Indian Ocean region were apprehensive of the great power military presence and rivalry in the Indian Ocean, because they felt that it could threaten their security and reduce their independent action. The idea of a peace zone in the Indian Ocean was mooted in the 1964 Cairo Conference of the Non-aligned countries and was given a concrete shape in the form of a resolution at the 1970 Lusaka Conference of the Non-aligned countries.

The Non-aligned countries in the Indian Ocean region were successful in getting the UN General Assembly to pass a resolution in December 1971, which called upon the members of the UN to make the Indian Ocean a Zone of Peace (IOZP) through the elimination of great power military presence conceived in the context of great power rivalry and competition. The 1971 UN General Assembly resolution on IOZP was mainly an approach towards peace in the region by insulating the area from the great power military presence, as majority of the littoral and hinterland countries of the region which were members of the Non-aligned Movement felt that peace could prevail in the region by the elimination of outside great power military presence in the Indian Ocean.[25]

Towards the end of 1960's, India took the decision to seek the co-operation of the countries in the region to make the Indian Ocean a zone of peace by insulating the area from outside great power presence. At the same time, India had also strengthened its naval capability. India, a non-aligned country, supported the Lusaka Summit resolution on Indian Ocean peace zone as it was in tune with India's security perception. Pakistan, an ally of the US, was in favour of the US presence in the region. Ironically, when the IOZP resolution was adopted by the UN General Assembly in December 1971, India and Pakistan were involved in an armed conflict ending up with the Indian army occupying the whole of East Pakistan. The dismemberment of Pakistan as a result of the conflict enhanced the fear of Pakistan about India in the South Asian region of the Indian Ocean. India, on the contrary, felt that outside military presence in the region, especially the US presence posed a threat to its security as it distorted the natural power hierarchy in the region. India strongly supported the 1971 UN resolution on IOZP as it felt that if implemented it not only ensures India's security but also enhance its power position in the region. India could effectively meet any threat from China, too, with the friendly help from former Soviet Union even if the Soviet forces withdraw from the Indian Ocean as the Soviet Union shares a border with China and the Sino-Soviet rift continues. Paradoxically, though Pakistan supported the IOZP resolution in principle, it desired the US military presence in the Indian Ocean as it felt that only the US presence would ensure its security. Though Pakistan was unhappy that the US did not prevent the dismemberment of Pakistan it felt that even the security of West Pakistan would have been endangered after the Indian forces had occupied East Pakistan but for the US clear warning to India not to proceed further in West Pakistan.

In 1971, when the UN General Assembly meetings discussed the IOZP proposal, Pakistan had raised the issue of the threat posed by India to its security.[26] Pakistan desisted from raising the regional issues in 1972 General Assembly meeting as there were some improvements in the Indo-Pakistan relation with the signing of the Simla agreement.[27] However, the Simla spirit did not last long and Pakistan once again reverted back to focusing on the threat from within the region, in the 1973 Ad hoc Committee on Indian Ocean meeting and the First Committee meeting of the UN General Assembly. In the Ad hoc Committee meeting Pakistan enthusiastically raised the issue of the regional threat to peace as the Committee was mainly constituted to find ways and means to implement the IOZP resolution with due regard to the security considerations of the littoral and hinterland countries in the Indian Ocean. During the initial period India's response towards the IOZP ranged from a strong support to the 1971 UN declaration as it envisaged the elimination of great power military presence in the Indian Ocean to a covert acquiescence to the Soviet thrust in the Indian Ocean in the absence of any progress towards the implementation of the declaration.

In 1974, the nuclear explosion conducted by India led Pakistan to introduce a parallel proposal to the Indian Ocean zone of peace in the form of South Asia as a Nuclear Weapon Free Zone (SANWFZ).[28] Pakistan maintained that the acceptance of its SANWFZ as the first step towards making Indian Ocean a zone of peace. Pakistan was successful for the first time in incorporating in the IOZP resolution of 1974 the necessity to look into the regional issues of the littoral and hinterland countries of the Indian Ocean. It continued to focus on the threat emanating from regional dominant power, India, and proposed a code of conduct to ensure an effective system of security within the Indian Ocean region. The code of conduct among other things, envisaged that military balance between dominant regional powers and weaker regional states should be maintained at a reasonable level in order to create an atmosphere of mutual confidence. India opposed the code of conduct and made it clear that any addition to the 1971 UN resolution on IOZP was unacceptable to it. In 1976, Pakistan termed the 1971 UN resolution on IOZP as impractical and undesirable and abstained from voting for the first time. [29] India while supporting the 1971 UN resolution on IOZP strongly opposed the continued US presence in the Indian Ocean. The divergent stand of India and Pakistan on IOZP reflected their contrary perception on security. India, as a dominant power in the Indian Ocean, considered the external power presence as a major threat to security of nations in the Indian Ocean region, contrary to this

Pakistan, a relatively weaker country in the region, supported external power presence, especially the US presence in the region.

A minor change in India's response towards the great power military presence was discernible when the Janata government came to power in 1977. The Janata government while following a 'balanced approach' opposed equally both the US and the Soviet military presence in the region. When General Zia-ul-Haq assumed power in Pakistan in July 1977 he reverted back to Pakistan's earlier stand of voting in favour of the IOZP resolution though it continued to harp on regional threat to peace in South Asia.[30]

The 1979 Littoral and Hinterland States Meeting in its final document incorporated the major items in Pakistan's code of conduct proposal, namely, the denuclearization of the Indian Ocean littoral and hinterland states, non-use of force and peaceful settlement of disputes, and agreements on the balancing of the military strength between the major littoral powers and the weaker regional countries. While Pakistan was happy with the inclusion of these items n the final document of the Littoral and Hinterland States Meeting, India was not in favour of its inclusion. India was against extending the territorial limits of the peace zone to the national boundaries of the littoral and hinterland states.[31]

The 1977-78, US-USSR talks on arms limitation in the Indian Ocean and the response of India and Pakistan towards at reflected once again the divergent approaches of India and Pakistan in making the Indian Ocean a zone of peace.[32] India supported the superpower talks on arms limitation and termed it as a step towards the eventual elimination of great power military presence from the Indian Ocean. Pakistan, contrary, to this, was opposed to the superpower talks on arms limitation as it considered that mere elimination of great power military presence or the limitation of it did not ensure the security of the smaller countries in the region against the threat emanating from dominant regional powers. Pakistan demanded the reduction of the military forces of dominant powers within the region.

The Soviet intervention in Afghanistan in December 1979 and Pakistan becoming one of the frontline states in the US counter-strategy to contain Soviet expansionism in the Indian Ocean region led to Pakistan's strong support to the US presence in the Indian Ocean. Pakistan felt that its security was threatened by the Soviet troops stationed in Afghanistan as well as the presence of dominant power India. India's silence on the Soviet action in Afghanistan intrigued Pakistan.[33] Hence Pakistan, in addition to the code of conduct demanded the Soviet troop's withdrawal from Afghanistan as a precondition to any initiative to make Indian Ocean a zone of peace. Unlike India, Pakistan was opposed to the early convening of the conference on Indian Ocean. India was concerned about the security threat posed by the militarization of the Indian Ocean and the US supply of sophisticated arms to Pakistan. Hence, India pleaded for an early convening of the conference on the Indian Ocean in order to implement the 1971 UN resolution on IOZP. By 1981, as the security environment in South Asia aggravated with the increased superpower involvement, India was even agreed to consider the security concerns of the smaller countries in the region, once the reduction of great power military presence in the Indian Ocean was achieved.

Despite change of government in India and Pakistan in 1985 and 1988 respectively, both governments continued to maintain their respective stands on IOZP without any change. India continued to maintain that the sole purpose of IOZP resolution was the elimination of great power military presence in the Indian Ocean. Pakistan, on the contrary, maintained that the SANWFZ and other items included in the code of conduct were the necessary preconditions to make Indian Ocean a zone of peace. These stands of India and Pakistan were also reflected in the 1989 NAM, Commonwealth and UN General Assembly meetings.[34]

During the cold war period India's major contention was that the great power military presence was the cause of regional disharmony and tension, hence it wanted the great powers to withdraw from the Indian Ocean. Pakistan's contention, on the contrary, was that the regional disharmony was the cause of great power military presence and hence it wanted the resolution of regional issues first, before considering the elimination of great power military presence.

Thus, it is clear that India tried to enhance its power position not only by supporting the elimination of great power military presence as envisaged in the 1971 UN resolution on IOZP but also by keeping its nuclear weapon option open. Pakistan supported the US presence as it perceived threat from India. Pakistan believed that a just solution to regional issues including the Kashmir problem based on the UN resolution can be possible only with the US support. The divergent stand taken by countries in the region also helped the super powers to continue and enhance their military presence in the region. Simultaneously the cold war situation as a result of super power rivalry also augmented the regional disputes.

The security situation in the Indian Ocean region during the cold war period was appeared to be based on three inter-related factors; first the asymmetries in the military power between intra-regional powers especially in the context of unresolved regional issues; second the outside great power interest and activities in the region; and third the interaction between intra-regional asymmetries and outside great power interests. In such a situation of mutual distrust among countries in the region any efforts towards peace would be an exercise in futility.

Peace and security in the Indian Ocean: The Post-Cold War Scenario

Peace and security efforts in the Indian Ocean underwent a major turn in the post-cold war period. The context in which the countries in the region initiated the IOZP has considerably been changed. The super power rivalry has come to an end with the disintegration of Soviet Union. However, a change in the international power structure, from bipolar system to unipolar/multiploar system,[35] does not necessarily ensure peace in the Indian Ocean. The threat perceived by countries in the region in the context of great power rivalry has been ended. However, the presences of the external powers continue in the Indian Ocean region. With the change in the international power structure, the threat perceptions of the countries in the region have also underwent a marked change. The post-cold war blurred boundaries between national security and international security on the one hand, and national security and human security on the other demands better cooperation among nations.

Peace and security in the Indian Ocean: US role in the Post-Cold War Period

The US policy immediately after the end of cold war was to ensure that no rival superpower is allowed to emerge in Western Europe, Asia or the territory of the former Soviet Union, the US is to maintain sufficient military might to deter any nation or group of nations from challenging the US supremacy and to prevent proliferation of nuclear weapons and other weapons of mass destruction and deter attack from regional forces.[36] This general policy of the US was well reflected in the Indian Ocean region also.

The geo-strategic environment in the Indian Ocean underwent a radical change in the early 90's due to two factors. One was the disintegration of the former Soviet Union which resulted in the formal end of cold war. The other was the Gulf war. As a consequence, all the earlier propositions of security in the cold war period have become totally redundant. The end of cold war has removed the necessity to attempt to prevent the negative consequences of superpower rivalry. Simultaneously the Gulf war shattered the illusion of regional security.

The Gulf war has left the US with the problem of protecting its security interest in the Persian Gulf for a long term. These interests include the continued supply of oil at a reasonable price, the security of the Gulf Cooperation Council (GCC) countries and the prevention of any single power from gaining control over the bulk of the Gulf oil resources and using the revenue to undermine the regional order.

In the cold war period a variety of strategies had been used to protect these interests. This includes reliance on the British presence in the region until 1971, support for Iran under the Shah until 1979 and support for Iraq during its war with Iran. The regional power equilibrium in the Persian Gulf was collapsed when the balance of power shifted decisively in favour of Iraq and the countries in the region were unable to pose a credible deterrent to Iraqi aggression. This necessitated the outside power intervention in the region to maintain status quo.

The US strategy after its punitive action against Iraq was to evolve a security system in the north western part of the Indian Ocean with all the six members of the GCC. The US also received cooperation from Egypt and Syria in maintaining a big force to ward off any threat from any quarters in the region. But they could not get much support from all the GCC member countries, as a few countries were reluctant to have foreign troops in the region. Finally, the US signed a 10 year agreement with Kuwait on 19 September 1991. The then US Defence Secretary, Dick Cheney told the US Congressional Committee in February 1992 that the US was going to expand its presence in West Asia and also its Rapid Deployment Force for swift decisive victory if the US has to fight against any third world country in the regional wars. Elaborating on his statement he further said ...in South West Asia we are striving with friends and allies to build a more stable security structure than the one that failed on 2 August 1990. But we have major interest in that part of the world and we must remain engaged to protect those interests. Therefore, we will increase our presence compared to the pre-crisis period. Hence we must be prepared to face adversaries on their term possibly involving the use of weapons of mass destruction and ballistic or cruise missiles. [37] This was the immediate strategy of the US to meet the post-cold war situation.

This strategy of the US had practical application in the region within a short span of time. The 11 September 2001 (9/11) terrorist attack on US world trade centre and the consequent Afghanistan war to do away with terrorism from there, and ensuing Iraq war to dethrone the dictatorial regime of Saddam Hussein, have demonstrated the US capability to intervene effectively in the region to protect its foreign policy objectives through coercive means. These developments marked the active and effective involvement of an external power in the region to maintain international peace and security in accordance with its own perception.

The terrorist attack on US had also rise two important questions, on the state sponsored terrorism and on the security threats to nation states from non-state actors. The international organizations are not well equipped in terms of military power and resources to effectively meet any challenges to international peace and security posed by non-state actors. In such a situation, US, the sole superpower in the post-cold war period, had taken over the responsibility to maintain peace and security in the region. The 9/11 attacks on the US attracted the attention of international community to wipe out terrorism from the region. The US led 'war on terror' once again legitimized not only the US presence in the region but also its active interventions. In the post-cold war period there was realignment and regrouping in the Indian Ocean region. The Indo-US relation improved further and India had entered into close collaboration with the US on defence and security issues.[38]

Inevitability of External Power Presence

The existence of international terrorism in the region in the post-cold war period, the shift in the international power structure from bipolar to uniploar, had also influenced the perceptions of countries in the Indian Ocean region about the external power presence. The sponsor of the IOZP, Sri Lanka now perceives the external power presence inevitable in the region. Likewise, one of the strong supporters of the 1971 UN resolution on IOZP, India has no hesitation to work in tandem with the US to monitor peace and security in the region. This change in the perception of countries in the region about the outside power presence made the 1971 UN declaration on IOZP a dead proposal. The emerging security situation appended with the accelerated pace of globalization demand better cooperation between regional and extra regional countries in the Indian Ocean region. It also demand ensuring national security by enhancing self defence capability, especially in the context of failure of global collective security mechanism to address threat to international peace and security posed by state as well as non-state actors and the existence of unresolved border disputes.

India's National Security and Indian Ocean

Indian Ocean is very important to India's military, economic, energy, environment, and human security. India has a coast line of 7516 kms and an exclusive economic zone (EEZ) of 2 million sq kms. The significance of Indian Ocean was predicted by Sir Alfred Mahan way back in 1890s he stated Indian Ocean as the Ocean which decides the destiny of 21st century. [39] The importance of Indian Ocean to India has long been recognized. India occupies a central position in the Indian Ocean region, a fact that exercises an increasingly profound influence on India's security environment. Writing in the 1940s, K. M. Panikkar, like Mahan, stated the importance of the Indian Ocean to India that;

While to other countries the Indian Ocean is only one of the important oceanic areas, to India it is a vital sea. Her lifelines are concentrated in that area, her freedom is dependent on the freedom of that water surface. No industrial development, no commercial growth, no stable political structure is possible for her unless her shores are protected.[40]

In tune with the above observations the first Prime Minister of India; Jawaharlal Nehru observed "History has shown that whatever power controls the Indian Ocean has, in the first instance, India's sea borne trade at her mercy and, in the second, India's very independence itself." [41] It was in pursuance of this idea India had supported the 1971 UN declaration on IOZP during the cold war period. In the post-cold war period also India had emphasized the strategic significance of Indian Ocean. This was reflected in the Annual Report (2004-2005) of India's Defence Ministry, which noted that "India is strategically located vis-a-vis both continental Asia as well as the Indian Ocean Region."[42] Again the Indian Maritime Doctrine asserts: "All major powers of this century will seek a toehold in the Indian Ocean Region. Thus, Japan, the EU, and China, and a reinvigorated Russia can be expected to show presence in these waters either independently or through politico-security arrangements." There is, moreover, "an increasing tendency of extra regional powers of military intervention in [IO] littoral countries to contain what they see as a conflict situation."[43] Accordingly, India framed its naval strategy in the Indian Ocean.

Maritime Security and India's Indian Ocean Policy in the Post-Cold War Period – elimination to engagement with external powers

Maritime security has become an important dimension of India's bilateral interaction with all Indian Ocean countries and regional organizations. Maritime security has become a multifaceted issue especially in the realm of nontraditional threat to security. The challenges in the field of nontraditional threat to security include maritime terrorism, smuggling transnational crime, drug trafficking and illegal immigration. In addition, the natural disasters oil spills and effect of climate change are threats and challenges that impinge on the national security of the Indian Ocean countries. The economic dimension of security challenges in the Indian Ocean region will become important in order to ensure security of vital trade routes particularly the choke points in the Indian Ocean.

In the post-cold war period, nations are very careful in their interaction with one another as the bipolar system ended. During the cold war period there was some kind of discipline among nation states imposed by the ideological confrontation. The international politics of the post-cold war is not the same in the cold war period. There is no ideological confrontation at the international level. Nations are more concerned about resolving their basic economic problem rather on pure military security. International cooperation is required for the protection and promotion of national interests, concerning peace, security and development. No nation whatsoever powerful can protect its national interest by pursuing an isolationist policy. This understanding among nations forced them to unite and work together to resolve domestic as well as external problems through international cooperation.

India's maritime policy also underwent a sea change in the post-cold war period. The policy of exclusive engagement and elimination of outside powers has given place to overt engagement with extra regional powers. This has been well reflected in India's joint military exercises along with the US, Japan, France, and Australia. India no longer considers the external power presence as a threat to its security. Rather it considers a joint effort is required to wipe out the major threat to India and international community posed by terrorism. It is not possible for any single nation whatsoever powerful to address the menace of international terrorism single handedly. India began to realize the importance of a realist approach in framing its foreign policy objectives and pursuing it through increased naval power and active collaboration with extra regional as well as intra-regional powers. This policy shift in India's stand is visible in the maritime doctrine as well as in the Navy's vision document published by the Indian Navy.

It essentially encompasses:

(i) Shaping a favorable maritime environment in the IOR for operations in peace as well as during conflict.

(ii) Preventing incursions by powers inimical to India's national interests by actively engaging countries in the IOR littoral, and rendering speedy and quality assistance in fields of interest to them.

(iii) Engaging extra-regional powers and regional navies in mutually beneficial activities to ensure the security of India's maritime interests.

(iv) Projecting the Indian Navy as a professional, credible force and the primary tool for maritime cooperation.[44]

India has also ear marked the area which falls within its immediate concern. "India's growing international stature gives it strategic relevance in the area ranging from the Persian Gulf to the Strait of Malacca...." While enumerating the basic features of India's post-cold war Indian Ocean policy "India has exploited the fluidities of the emerging world order to forge new links through a combination of diplomatic repositioning, economic resurgence and military firmness." [45]

India's Maritime Security Interests

India maritime security interests embraces the protection of India's vast coastline of 7,516 kms. India's maritime zones, over which it has certain rights and obligations, include a territorial sea up to 12 nm (22 kms) from the baseline, a contiguous zone from 12 to 24 nm (22-44 kms), an Exclusive Economic Zone (EEZ) from 12 to 200 nm (22-370 kms) and a continental shelf up to 200 nm. These zones currently comprise 2.013 million sq km area of sea which is the 12th largest in the world and equivalent to two-thirds of the total land area. India's has thousand-plus island territories and offshore installations. Again nearly 70 per cent of India's energy requirements of crude oil are currently shipped from abroad, increased focus would be required on the ability to maintain the safety and security of energy shipments and the prevention of any disruption of supply through multilateral cooperation. Another important maritime security interest of India is the prevention of maritime terrorism through multilateral efforts.

India's maritime interests are as follows: [46]

1. Protect India's sovereignty and territorial integrity against threats in the maritime environment.

2. Promote safety and security of Indian citizens, shipping, fishing, trade, energy supply, assets and resources in the maritime domain.

3. Pursue peace, stability and security in India's maritime zones, maritime neighbourhood and other areas of maritime interest.

4. Preserve and project other national interests in the maritime dimension.

India's Maritime Security - Aim and Objectives

India's maritime security aim is to safeguard national maritime interests at all times.

India's maritime security objectives are:-

1. To deter conflict and coercion against India.

2. To conduct maritime military operations in a manner that enables early termination of conflict on terms favourable to India.

3. To shape a favourable and positive maritime environment, for enhancing net security in India's areas of maritime interest.

4. To protect Indian coastal and offshore assets against attacks and threats emanating from or at sea.

5. To develop requisite maritime force levels and maintain the capability for meeting India's maritime security requirements. [47]

The task of providing security to the vast coastline, unlike the land borders, is a complex phenomenon involving multiple stake holders such as shipping, fisheries, offshore exploration and production, tourism, and scientific community. It is not only important to protect and promotes the multifarious interests of different stake holders but also involve them in the maritime security programme. Again many external factors that condition the peace and security in the Indian Ocean region have an impact on the maritime security of India. Therefore, any policy initiative towards maritime security of India is interplay of domestic factors and external factors. As far as the external factors are concerned it has less control. The success of India's Indian Ocean policy depends on framing a dynamic policy in tune with the external factors manifested and also considering the domestic prerequisites.

It appears that India has adopted a three pronged strategy to ensure maritime security through a more inclusive and pragmatic Indian Ocean policy. Firstly through diplomatic means, India has pursued a policy of cooperation with all major players in the Indian Ocean, including extra regional powers. This policy would help India to increase its international stature. The Indo - US strategic partnership in the Indo – Pacific region is an earnest attempt in this direction. The alliance of India, US, Japan and Australia, democratic countries initiative towards rule based ocean governance and free and uninterrupted SLOC and sea borne trade also attempted to deter any potential challenge to peace and security in the Indian Ocean from any corner that pay less heed to rule based Ocean governance. The process of globalization has also accelerated better and cordial interaction with outside powers as the movement of people as well as commodities would further cement relation between nations.

India has developed a friendly and cordial relation not only by bilateral exchange with nations but also strengthened the bilateral cooperation through interactions in regional organizations, such as ASEAN, EAS, SCO, BRICS, ASEM, IBSA, APTA, BIMSTEC and IOR ARC. India is vigorously pursuing the objective to become a developed nation by 2020. This requires the Indian economy to maintain an annual average growth rate of 8 percent per annum. India has framed the "Look East" policy and later the Act East policy in pursuance of this objective. Now the Act East Policy is a vital part of India's foreign policy. More than an external economic policy or a political slogan, the Act East Policy was a strategic shift in India's vision of the world and its place in the evolving global economy. It was also a manifestation of India's belief that developments in East Asia are of direct consequence to its security and development. Therefore India actively engaged in creating a bond of friendship and cooperation with East Asia that has a strong economic foundation and a cooperative paradigm of positive inter-connectedness of security interests. India becomes a member of the ARF in 1996 and considers it as an experiment in fashioning a pluralistic, cooperative security order reflective of the diversity of the Asia Pacific region. India is also a member of the East Asia Summit (EAS) which includes the ASEAN members and India, China, Japan, Republic of Korea, Australia, and New Zealand. It focuses on energy, environment, climate change, and sustainable development. The Act East Policy of India has included not only vigorous interaction with ASEAN but also improved relation with China. The ultimate objective was to evolve an Asian Economic Community on the lines of EU.

India has also pursued a policy of strengthening its economic and military power. It appears that in order to increase the national power India not only declared itself as a nuclear weapon power but also augmented its non-nuclear defense capabilities manifold. The maritime doctrine of India focuses mainly on building blue water navy.[48] India's role in ensuring the security of Indian Ocean region has been recognized by major players in the region mainly because of the major shift in its external policy through a pragmatic approach. As a result India was not hesitant to cooperate with any regional and extra regional powers. India has undertaken several innovative steps towards economic resurgence of the country. India's initiative to interact with nations at the bilateral and multilateral levels through various regional groupings appears to be based on this policy.

India's foreign policy has been adapted to the demands of the rapidly changing global, regional and domestic environments. The main drivers for reshaping India's foreign policy appears to have been the sustained dynamism of the Indian economy, emergence as a responsible Nuclear Weapon State, global expectations of India's role on the international stage and the capability to shoulder both regional and global responsibilities. India's engagement with the world community has grown to ensure a peaceful and supportive international environment that contributes to India's development goals. India advocates the need to evolve a new paradigm of cooperation, relevant to the contemporary world, in which global threats are addressed by global responses, and multilateralism becomes the preferred norm for addressing global challenges including terrorism, environmental degradation and economic meltdown.

Though India had made several strides in improving its relation with regional and extra-regional countries, the India - Pakistan relation still remain on distrust and mutual suspicion as it was during the cold war period. This shows the great power rivalry was not the sole cause for regional disputes though great power rivalry accentuated regional rivalry. Again the India – China border dispute also remain without a solution though China is India's largest trading partner. It shows that neither the unresolved bilateral political issues, nor the divergent political systems based on democratic and totalitarianism, are hindrance to economic relations between India and China. It also shows the growing significance of economic security rather than pure military security.

It appears that in the post-cold war period pure military security considerations has been replaced by economic security. The existence of non-traditional threat to security demands better cooperation among nations. The blurred boundary between international security and national security on the one hand and the national security and human security also demand better interaction among nations. In order to address the basic problems related to human security the countries in the Indian Ocean region has to come out of their cold war period mind set. Thus peace and security in the Indian Ocean region depends largely on better interaction among countries in the region and extra regional countries to ensure human security. In the post-cold war period any initiatives towards peace and security in the Indian Ocean region are dependent more on collaborations in economic security than on pure military security. The Indian Ocean Rim Association for Regional Cooperation (IOR - ARC) though a feeble attempt to establish economic community in the Indian Ocean, it is a welcome step towards stronger regional economic forum.

It appears that in the post-cold war period the initiative towards peace and security in the Indian Ocean is to be undertaken at three stages;

1. At the initial stage greater transparency is required in the economic and security relations among Indian Ocean countries.

2. In the second stage confidence building measures is to be undertaken at the bilateral and multilateral levels with the active involvement of extra regional countries.

3. Towards the final stage organizational set up to maintain peace and security through greater interaction among sub regional forums such as SAARC, ASEAN, GCC, and BIMSTEC.

Eventually maritime security of India depends largely on the security situation prevalent in the Indian Ocean region. Though the role of India in influencing the security situation in the Indian Ocean region is limited, it can play a leading role through diplomatic maneuvering. With the advent of accelerated pace of globalization, the emergence of nontraditional threat to the security of nations, the growing significance of human security concerns, it is imperative to address issues related to maritime security in a comprehensive manner. The blurred boundary between human security concerns and national security concerns once again necessitates such an approach. In short, maritime security of India is the interplay of domestic as well as the external policy preferences and responses. The national security predicament in the Indian Ocean region is very difficult to comprehend. It seems to be clashes of democratic values and totalitarian traditions and the divergent means adopted by them in addressing their respective national security concerns rooted in their respective domestic compulsions. Thus Indian Ocean offers both a challenge as well as an opportunity to frame India's maritime security policy.

Notes and References

1. UN Document. A/AC,159/1/Rev.

2. Ibid.

3. Standard Encyclopedia of the World's Oceans and Islands (London, 1969) p.161. Also McGraw Hill, Encyclopedia of Ocean and Atmosphere Sciences (London, 1980) p.200.

4. Ibid.

5. Ibid.

6. A detailed list of Straits and Channel in and adjoining Indian Ocean. See, UN Doc.A/AC.159/1.

7. Manorajan Bezboruah, US Strategy in the Indian Ocean New York, 1977 p.4.

8. LokSabha Secretariat, Indian Ocean as a Zone of Peace, New Delhi, 1979

9. Freedom to use the seas: India's Maritime Military Strategy, Integrated Headquarters Ministry of Defence (Navy) New Delhi,2007 p 25- 28.

10. In UN terminology 'littoral' applies to those of the Indian Ocean states which have a direct access to the Ocean or the adjacent Red sea and Persian Gulf, and 'hinterland' to the states which have no such access but are separated from the ocean by not more than one littoral state. See Segei Vladimirov "Indian Ocean Zone of Peace Conference – A Step Forward" New Times (Moscow) Vol.34, 1979, p.4.

11. Pakistan becomes a member of the NAM only in 1979.

12. R.Suresh, "NAM and Indian Ocean as a Zone of Peace" in N.Krishnan & S.Gabriel (eds.) Indian Ocean Problems and Perspectives for Co-operation Pondicherry, 1992 p.145.

13. Two-third of the World oil reserves is in Persian Gulf and Red sea, North-East African and Indonesia also have oil resources. The Indian Ocean region has around three-fourth of the total oil reserves of the world. The rest of the world mainly the developed countries are greatly dependent on the Indian Ocean region for oil. Studies showed that in 1976 the US imported about 38 per cent, Japan 75 per cent, UK 71 per cent, West Germany 78.3 per cent, and Italy 82 per cent of crude oil from West Asia. See Lok Sabha Secretariat, n.8, p.3.

14. Ibid., p.3

15. Ibid.

16. The countries in the Indian Ocean region mostly trade with the industrially developed countries of Western Europe, Japan, USA and USSR. The Intra-regional trade among them is comparatively very less.

17. Jawaharlal Nehru, the founder of India's Foreign Policy stated in September 1946: "In the sphere of Foreign Affairs, India will follow an independent policy, keeping away from power politics of groups aligned one against the other ....", See The Indian Annual Register 1946, Vol.II, Calcutta, Annual Register Office 1947, pp.252-253.

18. Indian Council of World Affairs, report on Defence Security in the Indian Ocean. (New Delhi, 1957) p.iii. K.M.Panikkar in his seminal work India and the Indian Ocean: An Essay on the Influence of Sea Power in 1945 argued that "the Indian Ocean must remain truly Indian" On the same line K.B.Vidya in his book Naval Defence of India, in 1947, argued that Indian Ocean can be an Indian lake if India is the Supreme and undisputed power over the waters of the Indian Ocean.

19. The Interim government had also recognized the necessity for a sufficiently strong naval force to guard India's long coastline and its sea-borne trade.

20. Lok Sabha, Parliamentary Debates 19 December 1963, Cols.56, 75, 67, 75.

21. At that point of time India wanted the US presence because in the Sino-Indian conflict US indirectly backed India. See. The Times (London) 10 November 1962 p.7.

22. See Rajya Sabha, Parliamentary Debates 18 November 1965, Cols. 1815-22.

23. The External Affairs Minister of India, Dinesh Singh stated: "We are against the setting up of any foreign bases in this area". Lok Sabha, Parliamentary Debates, 19 March 1969, Cols.3-5.

24. The External Affairs Minister, Dinesh Singh stated on 19 March 1969: 'Within the limitation of our resources we shall certainly take every possible step to safeguard our interest in the Indian Ocean". Lok Sabha, Parliamentary Debates 19 March 1969, Cols. 1-10; The Deputy Minister of External Affairs Surendra Palsingh on 18 December 1969 stated: "We want the Indian Ocean area to be made an area of peace and cooperation and any introduction of military forces from any side will be against our policy. We are also in touch with all the countries concerned about this matter and there is a great deal of identity views between us and the other countries". Rajya Sabha, Parliamentary Debates 18 December 1969, Cols. 4650-4653.

25. UN Resolution A/2832(XXVI)

26. UN Doc. A/C.1/26/PV.1849

27. As per the Simla agreement both India and Pakistan agreed that they would strive to resolve their outstanding disputes bilaterally.

28. UN Doc. A/29/PV.2247

29. The abstention of Pakistan was mainly to attract the attention of international community towards the threat emanates from within the Indian Ocean region.

30. SIPRI Yearbook of World Armament and Disarmament 1978 Stockholm 1979 p 474

31. India had always refers to the 1971 UN Declaration on Indian Ocean as a Zone of Peace.

32. Foreign Affairs Record Vol 24 No.3 1978 p134

33. Zalmay Khalizad, "Intervention in Afganistan Implication for the security of South West Asia", in William L.Dowly and Russel B.Trood

(eds.) The Indian Ocean Perspectives on a Strategic Arena (New Delhi, 1987), pp. 338-351.

34. NAM Doc. NAC 9/PC/Doc.1/Rev.3

35. According to Richard N. Haassit is Non polar system. The principal characteristic of twenty-first-century international relations is turning out to be non polarity: a world dominated not by one or two or even several states but rather by dozens of actors possessing and exercising various kinds of power. This represents a tectonic shift from the past.

36. Hindustan Times Sept 21 1991

37. The Times of India Feb 5 1992

38. For instance the Indo-US Civilian Nuclear Deal; Joint Indo- US Naval Exercises in the Indian Ocean

39. Suresh R, (2011) Peace in the Indian Ocean: A South Asian Perspective, Serials Publications, New Delhi

40. K M Panikkar (1945) India and the Indian Ocean, George Allen & Unwin, London

41. Quoted in Suresh R n.12

42. Annual Report 2004-2005 Ministry of Defence, Government of India, New Delhi 2005

43. Freedom to use the seas: India's Maritime Military Strategy, Integrated Headquarters Ministry of Defense, Government of India, New Delhi, 2007. Also see The Indian Navy's Vision Document, May 2006. www.indiannavy.nic.in

44. Ibid.

45. Ibid.

46. Ensuring Secure Seas: Indian Maritime Security Strategy, Indian Navy, Naval Strategic Publication (NSP), 1.2, October 2015, pp 9- 10).

47. Ibid.

48. Suresh R, India's Coastal Security: A Perspective in Dr C Vinodan (Ed) Defence and National Security of India: Concerns and Strategies, New Century Publications, New Delhi 2017.

India and the Indian Ocean: Strategic Security of Small Island Nations

N Sathiya Moorthy

By their very definition and geography, small island-nations have little or no control over their security. Swayed by the oceans and seas all round, and often with limited resources, including human resources, to man and master the seas from a security perspective, they also suffer from an inherent sense of insecurity *viz* their larger neighbours in particular. Such perceptions, not always justified but not wholly unjustified either, feed constant and continuing anxieties about their sovereignty and territorial integrity.

The Indian Ocean, like other swathes of water across the world, is dotted with islands, big and small. There are island groups as large as the Indonesian archipelago, and as small as Maldives, in the immediate Indian neighbourhood. In the immediate Indian context, Maldives and Sri Lanka, Mauritius and Seychelles, are small island-nations in the shared Indian Ocean waters. Their security also concerns India's security. Their sense of insecurity feeds India's security concerns, conversely.

Post-Independence India has had long and continuing political and security relations as much as it has been having economic and trade ties with both, from time immemorial. Often, the cultural relations between India and its island-neighbours, especially Maldives and Sri Lanka, are over-stretched to the point of adding new dimensions to their inherent anxieties about the larger neighbour devouring them one more time. Such concepts of 'cultural ties' may be considered for 'soft-power out-reach' between India and these two neighbours in particular, the results have been far from satisfactory. Hence, less said or stressed about them, the better for bilateral relations, especially over the medium and long-terms.

Inherent impossibilities

Over generations and centuries, small island-nations have invariably faced maritime and naval threats, real and at times imaginary. Either way, if these nations tend to belief that they are vulnerable to external threats of the kind, they tend to cover up in real and imaginary solutions. They tend to find allies in such external powers that they believe would be a bulwark against such other 'external threats'.

Often times, given the geo-political and geo-strategic conditions prevailing in their select and at times selective neighbourhoods, such 'external powers' also happen to be 'extra-regional powers'. Their presence and politics, their desire for dominance beyond their own seas and lands, tend to complicate matters even for those smaller island-nations, which had originally hedged their security concerns *viz* such other larger or smaller neighbours. The consequent complications become often too complex and too powerful for those small island-nations to face off, leave alone take on and neutralise as they might have desired and hoped for.

In context, these small island-nations, rather than playing one larger nation against the other (one of them possibly a bigger and powerful neighbour) find themselves in the cross-fire of those very powers. They may have their sovereignty and territorial integrity intact, but tend to lose a part of their decision-making powers and capacity, which are otherwise believed to be inherent to their sovereign powers.

Over time, such compromises to and on the sovereignty becomes the 'new normal' in their case, with the result, they as also their global play-pals tend to start off from that 'new normal' as the base for future negotiations and relations – rather than seeking to set the clock back on and to the 'real normal'. In such cases, the 'realistic normal' becomes the 'real normal', but that again keeps traversing and changing all the time. This is a factor that those small island-nations (as their continental cousins) tend to ignore at the start, but find themselves unable to reverse after a time.

A time soon comes when they are even unable to think about the 'real normal', which might have existed in another era, another generation, unconnected with theirs – and thus becoming 'unconcerned', too. Measured in context, the story of India's immediate smaller neighbours in Sri Lanka and Maldives, are no different. Rather, the India-Maldives-Sri Lanka trilateral can be a case study in relations between a larger power and its smaller, island-neighbours.

Sri Lanka: Recounting the past...

Between India's two immediate island-neighbours, Sri Lanka is the closest in geographical terms, and even otherwise. Sri Lankans –majority Sinhalas, and also minority Tamils and Tamil-speaking Muslims alike – do not shy away from identifying with India in historic, cultural and religious terms. The Sinhalas very readily acknowledge that they may have been sired by King Vijaya, who sailed from India. Even more relevant to the present day, Sinhala-Buddhist take pride in declaring at every turn that Buddhism went to the country from India, when Prince Mahinda, or Mahendra, and Princess Sangamitta, or Sangamithra, both children of Emperor Ashoka, took the religion to their land. The Bo sapling that Sangamitta had brought with her and planted in Anuradhapura in an era before Christ, continues to be a venerated place of worship for all Buddhists from across the island and pilgrims from across the world, to date.

The 'Sri Lankan Tamils', or SLT community, claims to be natives to the island-nation, formerly called 'Ceylon' at Independence (4 February 1948). Yet, when the 'ethnic issue' hit the young nation on the face, and more so when violence hit the Tamil streets and homes across the country, especially the most provocative 'anti-Tamil pogrom' of July 1983, they also began talking about an 'umbilical cord connection' with Tamil brethren across the Palk Strait, and the rest of India as their 'mother nation'. Such contradictions in their approach and consequent attitude towards the Sri Lankan State has also been among the various factors that have contributed to the 'ethnic strife' taking newer and uglier turn, from the late forties to the present-day. Of course, the main cause has been the inability and unwillingness of the 'Sinhala-Buddhist' majority polity and the community-dominated Sri Lankan State apparatuses to accept the SLT community as equal partners in post-Independence nation-building efforts, and their unabashed attempts, instead, to relegate them as 'second class citizens' within the larger Ceylonese imagery from the start, dating back to the pre-Independence political and constitutional initiatives.

There is the other, less-mentioned 'Tamil people', who are also 'lesser mortals' in the larger Sri Lankan politico-constitutional and socio-economic schemes. The Upcountry Tamils, or *Malayaha* Tamils', are descendents of indentured labour from the erstwhile Madras Presidency, who were/are mostly 'Tamil-speaking', to work the tea plantations under the shared British establishments in the two countries. While the British rulers, whose white brethren also owned those plantations, had no hesitation to 'import' those labour from a fellow-colony of the Raj, they did have problems conferring on generations of 'Indian origin Tamils', or 'IOTs' as they used to be known, unalienable rights as Ceylonese citizens. The idea did not even seem to have crossed the British ruler/plantation owners' minds, but then their post-Independence Sinhala successor rulers and owners went to the other end, to 'disenfranchise' them all and render them 'State-less', all at one go – and as among the early major decisions of the new dispensation. The irony is that the SLT political leadership of the time, apprehensive about the IOT numbers possibly outstripping their as the 'second largest community' in the country, voted for rendering the Upcountry Tamils, 'Stateless', when the issue came up before Parliament. Though they did split over the issue later on, there is nothing to suggest that the SLT leadership take up the cause of the Upcountry Tamils with the international community with the same vehemence that they did in their own case, later on.

If however, there is some political peace and constitutional space for the Upcountry Tamils to operate in the country even with limited socio-economic uplift over the past 70 years, it owes to the bilateral India-Sri Lanka Accords of 1964 and 1966, under which India as the 'mother-nation' accepted a certain percentage of IoTs as 'refugees'. Ironically, New Delhi's political initiatives, and also fiscal and military assistance in the cause of the SLT community with its confused and at times contradicting claims to an Indian/common Tamil parentage, has been much more compared to whatever India has done for the IOTs, over the past decades. Worse still should be the contributions of the Tamil Nadu polity and Government, both of which abided by the Centre's directives on the rehabilitation of the IOT refugees under the twin Accords of the sixties, without taking any political initiatives of the kind that they would do in the case of the SLT community and polity, including their better-placed Diaspora groups, in the subsequent decades, up to the present.

The fourth major 'ethnicity' comprises the island-nation's Muslim community, which is mostly Tamil-speaking, with a smattering of those that have an inherited sense of Sinhalese, or Malay identity in them. Unlike the other two Tamil-speaking ethnicities in Sri Lanka, their Muslim brethren have continuing blood and business relations with India, especially southern Tamil Nadu, since the pre-Independence past of the two nations. In a way, Islam came to both sides of the Palk Strait through Arab traders, who were anyway doing business with these parts long before the commencement of the Islamic era in present-day West Asia/Middle East. When the Arab community back home took to Islam, their brethren fully or half-settled along these coasts, from the days of erstwhile Tamil/Tamil Nadu kingdoms of the Cheras, Cholas and Pandyas to became Muslims. It was true of their brethren on the Sri Lankan side, too. Their trade and blood relations too flourished, and have continued to the present. A clearer picture of the Muslim presence and population-ranking in Sri Lanka would become available, if and only when the Government in Colombo releases the full details of Census-2012, undertaken after decades in the war-ravaged East and the North, where especially no decennial head-count was possible for three decades in a row.

...and living in the past

India's 'Sri Lanka problems', if they could be called so, earlier or now, owes to the average Sri Lankan understanding – or, misunderstanding – of the larger Indian socio-political dynamics, in the post-Independence era. Having over-simplified their cultural identification, or whatever of it, with northern and eastern India, where from they got Buddhism and Pali, the mother-language of Sinhala, the Sinhala-Buddhist of all ages and classes have made Bodh Gaya and Sarnath, as among their most favourite of pilgrim-centres. Those imageries of theirs are frozen in time, but on the politico-strategic sphere, they have related mostly to present-day Tamil Nadu, or what most of them, including the elite political class, continue to identify as 'south India'.

As Sri Lankan history goes – and chronicled in the sixth century Sinhala text '*Mahavansa*' – goes, a young Sinhala king, Dutugamunu had defeated an ageing Tamil ruler, Ellara, in a duel, after the two had honourably decided not to have their soldiers kill each other in a war. The *Mahavansa* also talks about how Dutugamunu had honoured Ellara after the latter passed on, but the subsequent generations have had little or no use for that part of the narrative. In short, the Sinhalas did not stop celebrating Dutugamunu's victory some 2,000 years ago, nor did the Tamils stop feeling humiliated about it over the same period, though no records of either seem to remain. So, when Rajaraja Chola and son Rajendra Chola, respectively captured northern Sri Lanka and the whole of the island-nation in their time, a full thousand years after the Dutugamunu-Ellara duel, the Tamil psyche did not stop celebrating and the Sinhalas did not stop feeling hurt and humiliated. The Sinhala hurt also had to do with King Vijaya, the founder of the nation, deserting his half-lion island-wife, Kuveni, and marrying a Pandyan princess from across the seas, from present-day south Indian State of Tamil Nadu. It is often said that Kuveni's curse is what has made Sri Lanka the troubled-spot that it has since become – though only in the past few hundred years, and more so in the past few decades since Independence.

It was/is not as much understood in India, starting with southern Tamil Nadu, that much of the ethnic-issue linked Sinahala/Sri Lankan misgivings about India owed as much to LTTE supremo Velupillai Prabhakaran choosing the erstwhile Chola kingdom's standard of a roaring Tiger as his militant outfit's symbol as to New Delhi's political engagement with various Tamil political and militant groups and also training and arming their youth, including the LTTE. That Tamil youth took to militancy only in their fight for self-protection and self-preservation after their moderate political leaderships had failed, against State-protected, if not State-sponsored Sinhala socio-political violence periodically unleashed on the SLT population, culminating in 'Pogrom-83'. In doing so, the Indian interlocutors could not, and hence did not link the present gesture of sending in medicine and other essential supplies to the Tamil civilians, 'under siege' by the Sri Lankan armed forces, in July 1987, as in the average Sinhala-Buddhist mind, it was possibly a repeat of the Chola naval armada from another era crossing over into their waters, and challenging their State structure and naval forces, which were nothing much to go by, in the twentieth century context of the shared Indian Ocean neighbourhood. In comparison, possibly the Indian Air Force (IAF)-centric *Operation Poomaalai'*, or 'Operation Garland', the humanitarian air-dropping of food, medicines and other essentials a day later, was a twentieth-century reality, whose initiation the Sri Lankan State and the Sinhala majority was unwilling to accept – and naturally so – though they were not as much unable to acknowledge, in the contemporary geo-strategic context of the times.

Maldives: Out from insulated isolation...

Compared to Sri Lanka, India's other Ocean immediate Ocean neighbour, Maldives, is still coming out of the insulated isolation from which it had derived both comfort and continuity for generations and centuries without break. Maldivians comprise descendants of indigenous people, as also traders from other parts of the Indian Ocean neighbourhood. There are claims that some of them might have been descendants of those from north-west India, those that had migrated from the forgotten Saraswat Valley. The local population was Buddhist by religious faith, and took to Islam when their ruler took to the religion, about a thousand years ago – a few centuries after the advent of Islam in the rest of South Asia, again through trade. A naval despatch of the Cholas from Sri Lanka is said to have visited the

Maldivian archipelago in an earlier century. Post-conversion, and without reference to religious beliefs, the Zamorin of Calicut, in present-day south Indian State of Kerala, has had stakes in parts of northern Maldives, continuing into/from the Minicoy Islands, which form geo-political part of present-day India.

Maldives had lived in tranquil isolation for much of its recorded history, until the Portuguese, based out of Goa, India, set sail, in the name of trade, a few hundred years ago. However, northern Maldivians, under Muhammad Thakurufaanu Al-Azam and his two brothers, successfully rebelled against the Portuguese, and threw them out of capital Male, where they were present for the previous 15 years. To the present, every Maldivian takes pride in their being the only South Asian nation not to have been colonised by a European power. The nation celebrates the exit as the Portuguese as the National Day of Maldives. During the Second World War, the Maldives became a Protectorate of the British, based out of and ruling Sri Lanka, but at least the locals seemed to have drawn a clear line. So, when in the mid-sixties, Prime Minister Ibrahim Nasir wanted to make the archipelago an attractive tourist destination, and the British based out of the RAF base in the southern Gan, would stand in the way, he had school students and other 'nationalists' to lend their labour during spare hours to broaden the runway of the Male Airport. Nazir then negotiated 'Independence' for the nation, and went on to become the President in 1968 – and continued in office for a decade.

Ibrahim Nasir was succeeded by President Maumoon Abdul Gayoom, who was in office for 30 years (1978-2008). He lost the first multi-party democratic elections conduced in 2008, under a new Constitution, to Mohammed 'Anni' Nasheed of the infant Maldivian Democratic Party (MDP). Nasheed 'quit' office before term, on 7 February 2012, following Opposition-led protests in which a section of the uniformed services participated. Vice-President Mohammed Waheed Hassan Manik, seen by many as a part of the Opposition movement, completed rest of Nasheed's five-year term, before Abdulla Yameen, half-brother of former President Gayoom, defeated the latter in a controversial election in November 2013. With Yameen reviving a pending criminal case against predecessor Nasheed, who then took political asylum in the UK after serving a short stint in Maldivian prison under local court order – and followed it up with the detention of other Opposition leaders, including Gayoom – the presidential polls of September 2018 saw him being replaced by MDP's

Ibrahim 'Ibu' Solih, a close confidant and long-time political aide of Nasheed.

Chinese 'debt-trap'

Though often ignored, there is a need to understand the social dynamics and political realities of nations like Maldives and Sri Lanka while studying their security concerns and strategic priorities. It does not stop with an understanding their strategic location advantage, which both States, for instance, have been 'exploiting' for since, and more visibly since the end of the 'Cold War'. With China as a new player most eager to woo and win them to its side, on its way to become the world's second super-power rivalling the US in the post-Soviet scenario, the Indian Ocean waters that both nations share with the larger Indian neighbour is not the same again. In a way, it was/is a continuation of the Cold War era dynamics but with the US' role reversed.

During the Cold War, the US was known to be wooing India's southern neighbours, and nearly succeeded in winning over Sri Lanka, then under President J R Jayewardene, on the presumption that India was already on the Soviet side. Post-Cold War, India and the US have moved closer, and have since formed the 'Quad' military arrangement, also involving Japan and Australia, to ensure 'rules-based' international behaviour in what they have identified as the 'Indo-Pacific'. China, rearing to go and pre-supposing the possibility of being choked out in the seas, off the Strait of Hormuz and the Malacca Strait, has been befriending nations around India, in what is called the 'String of Pearls'. This owes to the past adversity between the two Asian giants, namely, India and China, dating back to the 1962 war that the former lost, and Beijing's perception that New Delhi would be a thorn in its flesh as it plans for an era of exclusive Chinese glory from among the nations of Asia.

In wooing smaller nations, especially island-nations like Maldives and Sri Lanka, China has identified their needs and limitations, and has been seeking to address those needs, espousing and exposing those limitations. Individual Sri Lankans came out of geographical isolation long ago, and has been beneficiaries of the 'Gulf oil boom' first and shortage of trained house staff and the like across Europe, for decades now – and have been witnessed to the kind of 'infrastructure development' that they had helped create, with their own hands. Maldivians may have joined the race a little late, but the Nasir-invented, Gayoom-implemented 'resort tourism' economy put a lot of money in the hands of the individual, better education and foreign employment, even if only lately.

The consequent pressure on the ruling class in these two countries, especially in Maldives after it became a democracy, was too much for the inherent economy of the respective nations to bear. Under President Mahinda Rajapaksa in Sri Lanka (2005-15) and President Abdulla Yameen in Maldives (2013-18), China made big-time 'development investments' in the two countries, making them 'debt-prone' at the same time. For Rajapaksa's Sri Lanka, which had launched the final assault on an unrepentant Tamil LTTE, which was at the time considered among the most potent terror groups in the world, development was both a diversionary tactic and a socio-political necessity. There was need to create more jobs to keep the home-economy going, that too at a time when the rest of the world was already shaking under the 'global economic melt-down' and there were apprehensions of a massive cut in the forex reserves, where inward payments by Sri Lankan migrant employees constituted the single largest component. Sri Lankan State needed to make the world believe that all was well with the nation, war or peace. The Government also needed to carry the majority Sinhala people in particular with it, after earlier experiences, where war was often punctuated by the constant arrival of 'body-bags' to the Sinhala South – and nothing much else. When the rest of the world either was facing an economic crisis, and those that could invest were unsure of the security situation at the height of the LTTE war, China did put in the money where its mouth was.

The situation in Maldives was no different, when Yameen welcomed China with open arms. A self-styled economic visionary, President Yameen too was convinced that 'development is a substitute for democracy' and that more development would make the people's need for democracy that much less. Anyway, the infant Maldivian democracy, which was only five years young when Yameen took over, had already faced one cataclysm after another. There were also those inside the country and outside who firmly believed that western democracy would not serve Maldives, which had remained an unbroken sultanate for a thousand years – with its isolated, insulated population not knowing anything else, in turn, for a workable political administration.

In the mid-twentieth century the nation had experimented with an 'elected sultanate', which did not take off. Even the so-called elected Republican Presidents in Ibrahim Nasir and Abdul Gayoom acted as if they were 'elected sultans' of a different kind – within what could at best be 'democracy with Maldivian content'. As the first 'democratic' President, Nasheed faced the problems of personal and national readjustments, and it is safe to conclude that Yameen, when elected, sought to withdraw to the pre-democracy, pre-Nasheed times, but using the tools, texts and texture that democracy had offered in the interim. He did not find any contradiction in inviting big-time investments from China the same way Rajapaksa did in neighbouring Sri Lanka – both, without acknowledging, at least in public, that theirs was closer to the Chinese model of development than the western model of democracy.

The Chinese funding in Sri Lanka is believed to have pushed the nation into a 'debt-trap'. At least the incumbent Government of Prime Minister Ranil Wickremesinghe that succeeded Rajapaksa's said so, and settled for a 'debt-equity swap' with Chinese funding agencies for the controversial 'Hambantota Port project', which also involved a 99-year lease of a large chunk of Sri Lankan territory to them. At the same time, the Wickremesinghe Government only modified the terms of another controversial Rajapaksa era Chinese investment in the Colombo Port City project without cancelling it, as promised during poll-time. What more, it has also been borrowing in hundreds of million dollars more from China, for other 'development projects', like road-laying, where again all jobs continue to go to Chinese who are brought from mainland and not to local Sri Lankans, Sinhalas, Tamils or Muslims.

Post-Yameen, the new Government in Maldives has reiterated Candidate Solih's pre-poll promise of continuing to work closer with India, China and Saudi Arabia, which was the other nation that Yameen had relied on for development funding, including those of a religious kind, on his way to antagonising the closest Indian neighbour in every other way. Though Solih's MDP and party chief Nasheed had said otherwise, there is nothing on cards remotely seen as Maldives being able to pay back the China-debt or moving away from the 'Chinese sphere of economic influence'. This despite the fact that during President Solih's maiden overseas visit, to New Delhi, Prime Minister Narendra Modi, did offer a high $ 1.4-b aid to Maldives -- but not of course for repaying any part of the Chinese debt. Translated, it means that India could be trusted to extend all assistance to Maldives for future developmental funding, but the past scores, it would have to settle with China.

Security imperatives

Seen from an immediate Indian perspective, both Sri Lanka and Maldives may have moved away from the traditional 'India's sphere of influence' first, and fallen into a 'Chinese debt-trap', instead. As used to be understood, Indian 'sphere of influence' often related to 'strategic relations' while Chinese 'debt-trap' flows from excessive investment in the name of development projects which do not create more jobs or add to family incomes, but only give a gloss of prosperity while the foundations are sinking. What the Indian strategic community has forgotten through the post-Cold War era is that none of them, including those in the Government and thus being political leaders and policy-makers, have ever uttered the term 'Indian sphere of influence', which used to be a constant during the Cold War era. So to expect India's small neighbours to remember the Indian imperative from a forgotten past and act accordingly is just not on.

There is an additional reason for this. Though not Maldives *per se*, Sri Lanka, especially at the height of the Cold War and centred on the 'ethnic issue' nearer home, has perceived India with the kind of discomfort in matters of bilateral security arrangements, dating back to the 'Bangladesh War'. Earlier when India signed a treaty of friendship and defence cooperation with the erstwhile Soviet Union in 1971 and extended it by another ten years, it did not inform, leave alone consult, the southern neighbour, which suddenly found itself vulnerable, post-Bangladesh War. Post-Cold War, when India signed a similar defence treaty with the US in November 2005, Sri Lanka felt left out. In the Cold War era again, when Sri Lanka came up with a proposal for the UN to declare the Indian Ocean as a 'zone of peace', India at best was lukewarm.

Considering that Sri Lanka, a small island-nation, had everything going against in geo-strategic terms in the vast seas other than the location, including resources to defend itself against an aggressor, unilateral Indian decisions of the kind have often hurt the nation's pride and also sowed avoidable seeds of suspicion, about the future. The Sri Lankan experience with Indian agencies funding and training Tamil militant youth in the early eighties has unnerved all sections of the Sri Lankan State and the Sinhala society and polity, no end. Looking back from a 21st century global perspective, India's intervention of the kind, not only in Sri Lanka but also in present-day Bangladesh, flows from the UN doctrine on 'Responsibility to Protect' (R2P), but Sri Lanka and Sri Lankans did not, or do not see, it that way. Even when India sent the IPKF to Sri Lanka as a part of the Rajiv-Jayawardene Accord of 1987, Sri Lanka's strategic community and political leaderships continue(d) to see it only as a product of 'Indian misdemeanour' in the first place.

No such reasons or attributes are available to Maldives and Maldivians of the Yameen variety. Yet, flogging a larger neighbour, to whip up nationalist sentiments and/or divert the local population from immediate issues and concerns on hand, has been an age-old practice that has also worked in many, if not most cases. Before Yameen, half-brother, President Gayoom, had made vague references to India's Minicoy Islands being a part of Maldivian territory, centuries past. In his time, President Nasheed, even while proclaiming to be an unfettered friend of India, did touch upon the subject, but in a different way – and not in public. Nasheed presidential career came to an end only at the height of an anti-India protest, spearheaded by successor Yameen and others, in the name of wanting Indian infrastructure major, GMR Group, to exit construction-cum-concession arrangement for developing the Male international airport, renamed after Ibrahim Nasir in Nasheed's time. Through all these, the proponent-protagonists were playing up the inherent Maldivian pride of being the only South Asian nation not to have been subjugated by a European colonial power.

There is thus a need for India to re-visit old ties to the nation's geo-strategic ties with Maldives and Sri Lanka, and invest them with new understanding and comprehension, to make it all work. For instance, under President Nasheed, India and Maldives reworked their bilateral, bi-annual 'Dhosti' or 'Friendship' Coast Guard exercises by roping in Sri Lanka, the other Indian Ocean nation in the shared neighbourhood, but not other SAARC members. The Dhosti exercises itself flowed from India rushing military aid to Maldives to fend of Sri Lankan Tamil mercenaries who had sought to overthrow the Gayoom regime in 1988. Whatever the reason and justification, despite repeatedly asking India to withdraw the two helicopters, donated respectively by the Indian Navy and Coast Guard, during in final months in office, the Yameen regime in Maldives did not actually sought to effect it, or even risk it as such. Instead and at the same time, the naval vessels of the two nations did exercise together in the Maldivian waters. Maldives also sent back an India-donated vessel to Vishakapatnam for re-fit before it rejoined the Maldivian Coast Guard.

Bilateral strategic relations between India and Sri Lanka have even better, whoever ruled from New Delhi or Colombo. Standing aside, even the Rajapaksa regime granting permission for two Chinese submarines to berth in the Colombo Port may have to be viewed in context – not only as a part of the Government's 'five-hub plan' to boost the nation's economy but also as a friendly gesture to another friendly nation that too had stood by it through centuries, and through the decades of ethnic war, by meeting military requirements, where New Delhi was of little help after a point – and with full justification, which too was appreciated in Colombo.

The question thus remains if India too needs to take a stand-alone view of the nation's strategic relations with its southern neighbours and work on those strengths – rather than seeking to isolate them in the name of their Chinese connections and indebtedness, and feel isolated in the very same neighbourhood. For, if reports have to be believed, almost around the time India signed the defence cooperation pact with the US in 2005, Sri Lanka's bipolar political leaderships of the Sinhala majority, and also the Sri Lankan State, structure had taken a conscious and a near-consensus decision that in matters of larger strategic security, going beyond immediate internal security concerns even if of the LTTE variety, they would stand by India – rather, they would not entertain or encourage extra-regional powers, including the US, which Prime Minister Wickremesinghe dubbed the 'elephant in the room, which cannot be ignored'. Likewise, there also seems to be some understanding between Sri Lanka and Maldives on keeping extra-regional powers out of the shared Indian Ocean neighbourhood strategy, working with India, and India alone. The problem, if any, lies within the Maldivian domestic political leaderships. It is a concern that India needs to address.

Maritime Security: Search for New Institutional Mechanisms

Dr. Vibhuti Singh Shekhawat

Indian maritime security matrix is a complicated web of divergent strands such as British Colonial Legacy modern-day Indian bureaucracy, the clash between generalists and specialists, frequent policy announcements unmatched with suitable, commensurate action, role of fake strategic think tanks and collusion between multiple security agencies. The irony is that India still does not have an explicitly stated security doctrine which is the major drawback in addressing complex maritime security issues, within the existing system, nothing is hunky-dory and everything appears to be going haywires. While the population is expanding at an enormously fast pace, a large number of fragile eco-systems are getting diluted, disintegrated and ever decimated. Since all systems of mother earth are inter connected and serve as feedback circuits, one finds that marry species are either disappearing or imploding at an incredibly fast rate. This creates a dilemma for scientists, experts, policy planners and India's gloated bureaucracy space is getting shortened on the habitable earth. Scientists have formed panels and consultative groups to work out technical back up for study and deliberations.

The international maritime security landscape is unfolding events and changes in various ocean of this planet and Indian ocean, which is the mainstay of Indian maritime activity is faced with the problem of maritime security. Owing to big power rivalry and surreptitious entry of China, the threat to our maritime security has mushroomed to unheard of gigantic proportions. Our diverse and varied stands on security perception, coupled with bureaucratic pretensions to expertise, deadly toxic technologies and cynical negation of the maritime methodologies have added to our security concerns. What we have to evolve new are appropriate security concerns. What we have to evolve new are appropriate strategies and suitable mechanisms to meet the contingency. The employment of coastal guards and the straightening of land border through fencing surveillance equipments and sensors are good but not adequate to meet an emerging threat posed by foot soldiers and foreign navy personnels.

In view of this one may have to put added focus on maritime seascape whose contours are undergoing rapid changes that creates fresh vulnerabilities one must follow a time tested strategic culture. Strategic culture is defined by R.W. Jones as "a set of shared beliefs, assumptions and modes of behaviour derived from common experiences and accepted narratives (both oral and written) that shape collective identities and relationships to other groups and which determines appropriate ends and means of achieving security objectives."[1] Johnson defines it as "an integrated set of symbolic (i.e., argumentation structures, languages, analogies, metaphors etc.) that act to establish pervasive and long lasting grand strategic seem uniquely realistic and efficacious.[2]

These definitions are based on Indian civilizations, culture, geography and colonial experience during the British Raj. Based on this is the strategic doctrine which is a grand strategy of the nation which determines our security and defence policy formulation. This doctrine has undergone changes from time to time. These were a time when Nehruvian diplomacy held sways is which was perceived as a last resort to defend the nation. Nehru was a peacenik for whom peace was a passion and he worked on achieving lasting peace. As Shiv Shankar Menon has put is "our goals, must be defence, net offence, unless offence is necessary for deterrence or to protect India's ability to continue its own transformation."[3]

India still does not have a declared strategic doctrine. The Naresh Chandra task force was given work of formulating it and it submitted its recommendations in 2012. As matter of fact, our strategy has undergone several transformations and this is not surprising because the strategy of nation keeps changing and hence to keep pace with it, one may have to suitably amend and adjust our strategies also. In relation to Pakistan, it is "a strategic restraint and engagement" whereas in relation to China, is dissuasive defence. Narendra Modi has taken a mid-road between Indira doctrine and Gujral doctrine. The former was hegemonic intervention and the latter was restrained magnanimity. At the time of Doklam crisis, Modi took a firm stand and it paid. Obviously, we are gearing ground a policy of resolute firmness in matters concerning national security. This is also rooted in pragmatic realism. On the one hand, we are strengthening our border defences, on the other hand, we are also increasing our naval power in the Indian Ocean. We have to built a strong defence to meet the twin threats from China and Pakistan both.

Modi's strategy is a mix of strength and restraint. It is a comprehensive compendium of various strategies. Its stress is on making good relations with SAARC nations. Instead of Look East policy, he believes in Act East Policy. With Pakistan our relations are anything, but good because of continuous border firing and her proxy was in Kashmir with China it is a balance of hope and caution. Infact, we have to balance our closer relationship with UA and China. Russia continues to be our all-weather friend and we have close defensive ties with her. There is a distinct deepening of commercial ties with Japan to offset Chinese influence in the region. Our relation with South Korea, Taiwan, Vietnam, Thailand and Philippines are growing deeper. We have close commercial ties with them. We are also exporting Brahmos Missiles to Vietnam, to the great chagrin of China.

In short, Modi is trying to balance USA against China. We are having friendly ties with Sri Lanka and Maldives. Since Dragon is spreading its tentacles far and wide, we are also preparing an adequate response in countries of Africa and Australian continent. While not forgetting Europe, particularly France with whom we have defence ties styles also. India's role in BRICS rests on the assumption that the world is moving towards multipolarity.

All this has created new opportunities in the Indian Ocean which is no longer a British lake now and but is a competing ground for big power rivalry. To meet the growing Chinese threat in the region, India is steadily strengthening her maritime defences. Logistics today give an edge to us vis-à-vis China in the Indian Ocean and we are trying to capitalize on it. During Nehru era, our foreign policy was one of non-alignment and not of strategic thrust and authority. The commissioning of INS Vikramaditya and Arihant indicate our strong desire to strengthen maritime defence. We are adding a lot more platforms, weapons and sensors to argument our defence. A good number of submarines have been inducted into the sea. We have undertaken a programme of modernizing our ports and harbours. We are building mammoth ships and looking after the sealines of communication which are a major source of transport and safe movement of energy and other commercial products of import and export.

We have created Exclusive Economic Zone (EEZ) that confer on us the advantage of ownership of over two million square kilometer for harassing sea resources.[4]

The EEZ's in the Arabian Sea Bay of Bengal and around Andaman and Nicobar Islands enhance our control in our region. They are necessary to monitor exit and entry points in the Malacca straits[5] and have added a punch to our defence capability.

The high seas are no longer the patrimony of the big powers today. A lot of legal and illegal operations in including piracy has made this region vulnerable to foreign interventions owing to which, India has to create nodal agencies to coordinate with sea-based agencies such as Navy coastal guards and other shipping agencies. The regular Sea traffic from the straits of Hormuz and Malacca and is going importance day by day and hence one has to be vigilant and watchful. India uses sea police and other agencies to monitor it. The entry of China has made it a flashpoint. China I working on an alternate lard route to escape Malacca dilemma. The Karakoram highway linking the Gwader port in Baluchistan is intended to provide the alternate route to China. China wants to bypass the Malacca straits through which 90% of her trade is carried out. Already this place has reached a choking Point and China fears that in the events of war with, she would stall the entry of Chinese Vessels through this India has increased her surveillance in this area and put additional forces at Andaman and Nicobar shards which are strategically located.

South China Sea is yet another bone of contention among South Asian countries and China. China has reclaimed land areas is the Ocean and burled artificial islands where her military forces are stationed. She is threatening neighbouring states like Vietnam and Philippines to keep their military away from these areas because she claims exclusive ownership of this sea. India, USA and South Asian countries do not accept Chinese claims. High sea cannot be the property of one nation and navigation is open to all nations. Mary times USA has sent her warships in these region to war the Chinese that this sea is open to all.

Vulnerabilities

India is well placed in the Indian ocean as far as security and defence scenario is concerned. But still, it is not totally secure because of Chinese advances into it. Only on January 10, 2017, Indian television beamed the rather discomforting news that China has sent many naval ships in the Indian ocean region, ostensibly to fight the pirates but the real intent is to create a ring round India from Malacca strait to Srilanka and Maldives in the Arabian Sea. The Chief of the Indian Naval Staff has already voiced concern at the growing Chinese presence in the Indian Ocean. Already

China is investing a huge sum of 43 billion US dollars on the old silk route and in the Indian ocean and attracting small neighbours with prospect of economic investment. Many small countries in the neighbourhood have evinced great interest in the project. Pakistan has been totally sucked into the Chinese economic orbit and in the years to come, will not come out of it. But not every country is enthused about China's economic bail. India has resolutely refused to be a part of this project whereas Malaysia and Indonesia have their own reservations. Vietnam and Philippines too are shaky about it. The reason is obvious China is keen to extend its sphere of economic influence and has taken a long term economic view of imposing economic thralldom for on countries that think that Chinese bounty would bring indirect investment in their blue economy.

Piracy is another cause of concern particularly off Somalia. Somalia has become a haven for piracy. Several factors have led to an increase in the incidence of piracy here. These are growing unemployment, bad governance, poaching by foreign fishing vessels and indiscriminate dumping of toxic waste in the waters of Somalia. Hence piracy has become a convenient means of livelihood for the pirates of Somalia. There have been incidents of seafarers being held hostages for huge ransom, which causes great psychological and actual trauma to these held in captivity.

Presence of extra region powers like USA and China in Indian ocean has made this an arena of sabre-ratting, India suggested in the Galle conference at Sri Lanka that Indian ocean be made a Zone of peace. This is necessary to save energy requirements of countries in this region. US have already deployed her fifth fleet from the Middle East with ships deployed at Bahrain. The discovery of shale gas in the area has increased US interest because this will reduce US dependence on traditional energy resources. The USA has already declared its intention to moorage the number of units in Middle East by 25% which indicates net only renewed US interest in the region because of energy needs but also owing to geopolitical factors such as China's increased activities here which poses a direct challenge to the countries situated he. China, efforts to seek new footprints here is a causal worry for every state including USA and India.

It is interesting to note here that China is investing huge sum at Hambanthota in Srilanka and is likely to use it as a military base. Sri Lanka had first made an offer to India to invest here but because to policy paralysis, she dilly dallied and finally, China got the lease of this strategic part.

Because of these manifold challenges, there is urgent need for creating new institutional props and mechanisms to make our foreign policy pragmatically realistic. It is a happy sign that the new government is freed from the previous government's policy paralysis syndrome and is recasting foreign policy objectives to keep them in tune with new emerging realities. India is investing a lot of defence, particularly in its Navy strength which augurs well for the future. In particular, we are stabilizing our maritime neighbourhood which focuses on Chinese machinations. We are now earnestly maintaining the security of sea lanes so as to facilitate uninterrupted sea trader and transport. We have already been increased our amphibious capability and created a fleet of nuclear submarines to protect our coasts and deliver a devastating blow to any adversary who chooses to engage us in a nuclear war. We have adequately increased the strength of our Coast Guards and Coastal Security Group for increased national security. In short, we now have a credible underwater force which is strong enough to deliver powerful blows to an enemy who challenges as first in any type of war-conventional or nuclear.

Reference

1. R.W. Jones (2006), India's Strategic Culture, p.4.

2. Quoted by K Bajpai, Indian Strategic Culture, taken from Suresh R (ed.) The Changing Dimensions of Security Vij Books India, Pvt. Ltd., Delhi, 2015, p.27.

3. Ibid., p.29.

4. Ibid., p.173.

5. Ibid.

Maritime Security of India: A Military Perspective

Brigadier Suresh Nair

Introduction

A look at the map of India here in the context of the Asian Sub Continent gives a fair idea of the immense importance of oceans to it, its positioning in the Asian sub-continent gives it tremendous geographical advantages, clearly underscoring the importance of maritime security to India's wellbeing. But Indian policy makers have been mainly land centric and have harped on the importance of protecting its land borders, of course with sound reasons too. India has the unique distinction of being the only country facing two adversaries both on the Western and Eastern borders. On our Western flank we have a sworn enemy in Pakistan and a powerful rival China along its Northern and Eastern borders. We have a long border with China with whom we had a border war in 1962. Though peace and tranquility by and large prevails, there have been many dangerous military standoffs, the last prominent one being in Doklam on the Sikkim front in 2017. We have fought four wars with Pakistan where the army calls all the shots especially when it comes to defining its relations with India. It has a military doctrine ` to bleed India with thousand cuts' through a set of non-state actors a la terrorists actively fermenting unrest in the Kashmir valley to force its accession to Pakistan. This is enabled through infiltration of terror groups which keeps the Line of Control (LoC) literally on fire. Concurrently, it has also developed close relations with China. It serves the purpose of China to prop up Pakistan, to tie down India's ambitions of being a global player. Thus it is quite justifiable that India's land borders and its defence has been an obsession with Indian policy makers and cannot be neglected.

But just as China has understood that the future lies in the Oceans and have made giant strides towards that goal, India too has realized the importance of its vast surrounding oceans and have started emphasizing on the need to enhance its maritime capabilities in the Indian Ocean region and beyond, though may be in a lesser scale than that of China.

Maritime security not only involves protection of one's Exclusive Economic Zone (EEZ), but also ensuring freedom of navigation in international waters. It is also just not the physical protection of the seas; it encompasses a vast canvass from protecting the Trade which is linked to the overall economic wellbeing, infrastructure development of ports/harbours, fishing industry, shipbuilding etc., and there are also diplomatic and military aspects to it. Coastal security also assumes huge importance in the light of terrorism, especially after 26/11 Mumbai attacks. I will confine myself to some military aspects of maritime security.

Significance of Indian Ocean Region (IOR)

"Whoever controls the Indian Ocean dominates Asia. This ocean is the key to the seven seas in the twenty-first century, the destiny of the world will be decided in these waters".

– Rear Adm Alfred Thayer Mahan, US Navy Geostrategist

Alfred Mahan, Great American naval strategist described Indian Ocean as the most important and strategic Ocean in the twentieth century, and with the present geopolitical situation, his words are coming true, as most of the economic interests of the world are routed through this ocean. For emerging economies, India and China, IOR region is very important as their energy resources, which are essential for their economic growth, route through the sea lanes of communications (SLOCs) in the Indian Ocean. The Indian Ocean affords direct access to the Indian landmass and it constitutes an intrinsically significant security area to India, whereas it is only extrinsically important to other states. For India, the Indian Ocean is even more important as any external military presence can pose serious security challenges to the nation. New Delhi regards the Indian Ocean as its backyard and deems it both natural and desirable that India functions as, eventually, the leader and the predominant influence in this region-the world's only region and ocean named after a single state. For India, the Indian Ocean is also very important for projection of its power in world's politics.

The Bab el Madeb strait between Djibouti and Yemen, the Hormuz strait between Iran and Oman, and the Malacca strait between Indonesia and Malaysia are the three critically important entry and exit points in the Indian Ocean. About two-thirds of Gulf oil exports go to Asia across the Indian Ocean. Unlike the Atlantic and Pacific Ocean, the Indian Ocean is a comparatively closed area and access to it is possible only through the choke points. Therefore the Indian Ocean can easily be controlled by controlling these choke points. More than 70% of our hydrocarbon comes from the Persian Gulf and ensuring energy security is strategically paramount. From a security perspective we have to ensure that our trade routes which pass through the Indian Ocean should not get disrupted.

There is considerable geopolitical turbulence in the Region—the tensions in the Korean peninsula with an unpredictable and aggressive North Korea,territorial disputes with China in the East and South China seas and its enhancement of the infrastructure in the disputed SCS islands have risen the temperatures within the region as also with the US. As a result, the maritime security environment is undergoing pivotal shifts with unprecedented modernisation and expansion of regional navies.

China's Consolidation strategy in the IOR

China adopted a new policy of "Building a Strong Maritime Country", as China's land borders are relatively tranquil, the unresolved Taiwan issue and complex maritime disputes with six neighbours have led to enhanced focus on sea-power. China's leadership has astutely grasped that to be a world power it has to have long reach and that 'maritime power' is much more than just a 'fighting navy'. The results are truly striking; China is today the world leader in ship-building and its 5,000-ship strong merchant marine ranks No.1 in the world.

China's strategy to secure its interests in the IOR consists firstly of its expansive Belt and Road Initiative, which also has a maritime component, known as the "Maritime Silk Road". Next is a major naval modernization programme including development of force projection capabilities and thirdly obtaining greater access to ports in the Indian Ocean. Chinese shipyards are rapidly adding to its fleet of modern warships as well as merchantmen. Its force of home-built nuclear submarines is operationally deployed, As of 2018, the People's Liberation Army Navy (PLAN) has a single combat-ready aircraft carrier, the *Liaoning*, with a second and third under construction. It is projected that China may possess up to five or six aircraft carriers by the 2030s and by 2020, the PLAN will overtake the US Navy in numbers, and remain at No.2 only in capability.

The Chinese leadership has long been haunted by the spectre of the "Malacca Dilemma"-the notion that its trade and energy supplies flowing through the straits can theoretically be cut off by an unfriendly power. While analysts have cast doubt on the practicality, operational feasibility, and strategic effectiveness of mounting a blockade of the Malacca Straits, this "dilemma" is still cited by Chinese analysts as China's primary security threat in the Indian Ocean. Possibly as a way to overcome this problem, China has launched the China Pakistan Economic Corridor (CPEC)—a land transport corridor linking Gwadar on the Arabian Sea to the Chinese city of Kashgar. Many analysts, however, are skeptical of the viability of CPEC as an alternative to the Malacca Strait Chinese dilemma and still are of the opinion that the sea routes will remain critical. The CPEC and in particular Chinese access and control of Gwadar port are of great concern to Indian security interests.

With Sri Lanka's Hambantota port which has been officially transferred to China In August 2017, commissioning of its first overseas naval logistics base at Djibouti and control of Gwadar Port in Pakistan, China has gained immense strategic advantage as part of its so called `string of pearls strategy'.Latest reports indicate Chinese consolidation in Colombo port too. A China-funded port city being constructed in Sri Lanka's capital Colombo will soon be ready for the second phase. The mega 1.4-billion-U.S. dollar is co-developed by the Sri Lankan government and China's CHEC Port City Colombo (Pvt) Ltd under the Belt and Road Initiative. A major stake holder of CHEC is the Chinese Govt.

It can be seen that China is consolidating in the IOR at an incredible pace. However, In order for China to use these facilities for effective military purposes, it should build a navy which can project power far from its shores. Though there are many hurdles to Chinese expansion it is clearly well on its way to do so.

India's Indian Ocean Strategy

India's response to these developments has been to develop closer ties with the United States and its allies—primarily Japan and Australia. India has embarked on an unprecedented partnership with the US. As China's rise and perceived aggressiveness threatens both U.S. and Indian interests—this relationship is only expected to further strengthen. In addition, India has enhanced its links—including defence ties—with both Japan and Australia.

In the IOR, the Japanese government has expressed interest in assisting India in the development of the Andaman and Nicobar Islands—a further cause of consternation for China. India's recently declared Act East Policy is to a large extent linked to the concern for security of this region.

India's maritime security strategy towards East Asia

In the context of India's maritime security strategy towards East Asia, given the larger than life presence of China in the Region, India must remain flexible and discreet in its engagement with Southeast Asia. Other than Singapore which historically recognised India as being a natural security provider and Vietnam with whom India has revived its links in recent years, India will need to develop other partners in the region, some of which have been more hesitant in recognising India's regional security role. India's most important potential partner is Indonesia, which has the potential to transform India's regional role.

India's Leading Maritime Security Role in the Northeast Indian Ocean

India has a leading maritime security role in the northeast Indian Ocean, as a function of its geographic advantages and relative capabilities. In recent years, India has been reinforcing its capabilities in the northeast Indian Ocean. Much of India's naval modernization program over the last decade has focussed on improving its capabilities in the northeast. There has been a considerable "rebalancing" of defence resources from the Indian Navy's Western Command to its Eastern Command.

India's dominant strategic position in the northeast Indian Ocean is underpinned by its possession of the Andaman and Nicobar islands in the Andaman Sea near the western end of the Malacca Strait. These islands also form a natural base for India to project power into the Malacca Strait and beyond into the South China Sea. They have been described by a Chinese naval writer as constituting a "metal chain" that could lock the western end of the Malacca Strait tight.

With modern aircraft carriers, along with potent surface, sub-surface and air platforms, Indian Navy has more or less a balanced force capable of undertaking a range of operations, from the brown to the blue waters, and also contributes to regional security. The Indian Navy last week commissioned a new air base -- INS Kohassa -- in the Andaman and Nicobar islands as part of efforts to expand operational presence in the Indian Ocean.

Highlights of Indian Navy's Maritime Security Strategy

In keeping with the aspirations of India's growth story and its increasing importance globally, India's Maritime Security Strategy has expanded its scope in its maritime interests.

Primary Areas

India's primary areas of maritime interest include the following:-

- India's coastal areas and maritime zones, including coastline, islands, internal sea waters, territorial waters, contiguous zone, EEZ and continental shelf.

- The Arabian Sea, Bay of Bengal, Andaman Sea, and their littoral regions.

- The Persian Gulf and its littoral, which is the source of majority of our oil supplies and gas imports, and is home to more than seven million expatriate Indians.

- The Gulf of Oman, Gulf of Aden, Red Sea, and their littoral regions.

- South-West Indian Ocean, including IOR island nations therein and East Coast of Africa littoral regions.

- The choke points leading to, from and across the Indian Ocean, including the Six degree Channel; Eight/ Nine-degree Channels; Straits of Hormuz, Bab-el-Mandeb, Malacca, Singapore, Sunda and Lombok; the Mozambique Channel, and Cape of Good Hope and their littoral regions.

- Other areas encompassing our Sea Lanes of Communications (SLOCs), and vital energy and resource interests.

Secondary Areas

India's secondary areas of maritime interest include the following:-

- South-East Indian Ocean, including sea routes to the Pacific Ocean and littoral regions in vicinity.

- South and East China Seas, Western Pacific Ocean, and their littoral regions.

- Southern Indian Ocean Region, including Antarctica.

- Mediterranean Sea, West Coast of Africa, and their littoral regions.

- Other areas of national interest based on considerations of Indian diaspora, overseas investments and political relations.

Indian Maritime Security Strategy, revised in 2015 has accorded increased focus on the following:-

a. The safety and security of seaborne trade and energy routes, especially in the IOR, considering their effect on global economies and India's national interests.

b. The importance of maintaining freedom of navigation and strengthening the international legal regime at sea, particularly the United Nations Convention on the Law of the Sea (UNCLOS), for all-round benefit.

c. The considerable scope and value in undertaking cooperation and coordination between various navies, to counter common threats at sea.

Indian Navy's Maritime Security Strategy does not envisage hedging against any country. Unlike land borders, international waters do not have any borders and is open for use by global commons, therefore to suggest that we should match our capabilities with that of China or any other nation may not be valid. One look at the vastness of the Indian Ocean Region will reveal that it will be foolish to even try that.

There are areas of non-traditional threats like Human Assistance during disasters, Piracy, Theft, Seaborne terrorism, narcotic and human trafficking etc which the Indian Navy has taken the lead in the Region with active cooperation of other countries. The prospect of disruption of trade at critical chokepoints, such as the Strait of Hormuz or Malacca, can be catastrophic for the global economy. Maintaining unimpeded flow of energy and other commodities over the sea is therefore a prime concern for all nations, including ours. The Navy deploys its assets at all choke points which are inlet to IOR 24x7. All ships, aircraft and submarines are on the task and from virtually all naval bases of the country including Andaman Nicobar Islands.

Regional relationships most notably with Japan and Vietnam — as well as developing ties with the U.S. Navy — will form the bedrock of Indian maritime strategy.

It also needs to be remembered that China, Japan and South Korea have around same percentage of their oil coming from this area and to imagine that China will disrupt oil flow in this region is not a possibility because China's own vulnerability and dependence on hydrocarbon from here. While It may never be in India's interest to counter China, either in home waters or abroad; my own prescription is that China and India have no choice but to cooperate in maritime arena particularly in the IOR. No one country in the world can ensure Maritime Security of Oceans. It has to be collective arrangement or else US would not have slowed down.

Basic principles for pursuing maritime security initiatives

Should encompass the following:

    a.   Full respect for sovereignty of littoral states

    b.   Maritime security is a common cause

    c.   Maritime security is not the sole responsibility of littorals alone. Everyone plying these waters has a stake and role in its security.

    d.   Consensual and collaborative approach in all initiatives as per international law

    e.   Cooperative response in the event of natural calamities or major incident at sea.

Conclusion

There are clear indicators that India is prepared to take on more active role in the Indo Pacific Region, which no doubt is precipitated by the rise of China and its growing influence in India's backyard ie the IOR.. Not only it is essential to have enhanced naval capabilities, more importantly India's land centric mind set has to change; the traditional mentality that land outweighs sea must be abandoned. Our geographical strengths in the maritime sphere should be exploited. Importantly, there should be a carefully thought-out, overarching maritime master plan as part of National Strategy for Maritime Security. Navy, by itself, constitutes just one component of the country's maritime capability. Without the remaining elements, India's maritime power will remain hollow. India's ports and infrastructure remain backward, our shipbuilding industry is stagnating, fishing industry, sea bed mining, merchant fleets are all far behind. All these need a fillip to develop an all-encompassing Maritime Strategy which then would be more suited to support our active Maritime Security Policy.

The Evolution of China's Maritime Security Strategy and Sino-Indian Maritime Security Relations

Huo Wenle

Abstract

Since the independence in 1949, China's maritime security strategy in the Indian Ocean region has evolved three phases: Phase I, from 1949 to mid-1980s, China could not sustain naval presence in the region due to severe security pressures and limited power projection capabilities; Phase II, from the mid-1980s to 2008, China started and increased its naval presence in the Indian Ocean region; and Phase III, from 2009 to till date, China have achieved permanent presence due to the anti-piracy patrols in the Gulf of Aden and its opening of first overseas military base in Djibouti. Sino-Indian maritime cooperation in the Indian Ocean region includes official visits, ship visits, joint maritime drills and exercises, anti-piracy cooperation, and maritime affairs dialogue, etc. To be sure, Sino-Indian maritime security cooperation is limited now in terms of scope and depth, which reflects the mistrust between China and India. Both China and India are suspicious about each other. China believes that India intends to dominate the Indian Ocean and concerns Indian close maritime security cooperation and coordination with major powers such as United States and Japan, while New Delhi is apprehensive about China's so called 'String of Pearls' strategy, military involvement into the Indian Ocean Region and China's Maritime Silk Road Initiative. Given the mutual nuclear deterrence, economic interdependence and the geopolitical characteristics of the Indian Ocean Region, there is a small chance for China and India to have military conflicts in this region. However, because of the lack of mutual confidence, especially in the strategic and security fields, it is imperative for China and India to further enhance bilateral cooperation on maritime security. Such activities include increasing high level official exchanges, warship port visits, joint training and exercises bilaterally and multilaterally, positive cooperation in tackling piracy in the Gulf of Aden, and conducting regular consultations on regional maritime security through effective maritime cooperation dialogues.

Evolution of China's Maritime Security Strategy

The evolution of China's maritime security strategy in the Indian Ocean Region (IOR) from its independence in 1949 to till date can be divided into three distinct phases: Phase I, from 1949 to mid-1980s; Phase II, from the mid-1980s to 2008; and Phase III, from 2009 to till date.

Phase I, between 1949 and mid-1980s

During this period, the severe international and domestic situations facing China had greatly constrained its maritime outlook. On one hand, the world was experiencing the Cold War which was characterized by bipolar pattern between the United States (US) and the Soviet Union. While the U.S.-led capitalist camp carried out political isolation, economic sanctions and military containment against China in the 1950s, Beijing proposed the diplomatic strategy of 'leaning to one side' to ally with the Soviet Union-led socialist camp. On the other hand, China's inward-looking policies caused China paying more attention to national security regarding national unity, territorial integrity and prevention of foreign aggression rather than maritime security. There are some reasons contributing to this. Given the bipolar confrontation pattern and inward-looking policies, China had not yet developed an outward-looking economy successfully as it did in the next phase, which made China lack of economic motives to develop powerful ocean-going navy to protect its overseas interests. In addition, for a long time after China's independence, the Chinese People's Liberation Army (PLA) Navy had to pursue the maritime security strategy of coastal defence, because of its security situation and limited naval power. The weak PLA Navy had to defend the severe threats from 'the Kuomintang fleet with 150 warships and the US Seventh Fleet' (Cottrell and Burrell 1976: 502). Therefore, China had 'neither the ability nor the intention' to establish a maritime force that can be able to conduct long-term operations in the high seas (Cottrell and Burrell 1976: 502).

Regarding China's maritime security strategy in the IOR, China had maintained its limited presence in this region mainly through political, diplomatic and economic approaches, rather than military method. In the early 1950s, Sri Lanka helped China break the US embargoes through the rubber-rice pact. Although economic and technical assistance, as well as the bilateral trade agreements with states in the IOR contributed to China's influence in this region, the Indian Ocean was far from an important channel for China's trade. China also endorsed the resolution of *Declaration of the Indian Ocean as a Zone of Peace* passed by the UN General Assembly held in December 1971, which was welcomed by most states across the Indian Ocean region. In addition, China also tried to show its presence in the IOR through limited military assistance to several countries, Pakistan in particular. However, this phase never experienced PLA Naval physical presence in the Indian Ocean region. As noted above, it is not difficult understand 'any sustained Chinese presence in the IOR was only peripheral' during the period between 1949 and the mid-term of 1980s (Kondapalli 2018: 119).

Phase II (between the mid-1980s and 2008)

This period has experienced the transformation of China's naval strategy from coastal defence to offshore waters defense and also witnessed the PLA Naval increasing presence in the Pacific and the Indian Ocean regions.

During this period, major changes have taken place in the international and domestic situation. The Cold War came to an end with improved US-Soviet relations in the late 1980s and ended with the dramatic changes of Eastern Europe and the collapse of Soviet Union in the early 1990s, which not only led to the rapid reduction of the security threats China facing from the Soviet Union and the US, but also resulted in the speed up of the globalization process. After the reform and opening up policy initiated in 1978, China's economy grew rapidly with the increase and development of maritime trade, demanding maritime resources and overseas investment and assets, etc. In other words, China's overseas maritime interests have expanded rapidly from the Pacific Ocean to the Indian Ocean and beyond, especially after China joined the globalization process and World Trade Organization (WTO) in 2001. However, with the expansion of its overseas interests, China has gradually realized its vulnerability to maritime security challenges ranging from national reunification, maritime disputes and major power struggles in terms of traditional security to piracy, maritime terrorism, natural disasters in terms of non-traditional security. With the Taiwan issue still being the core and primary issue of China's strategy, its maritime disputes with other states or parties were emerging in this period. The 11/9 event in 2001, rising piracy threat in the South China Sea and Northwestern Indian Ocean region, and the multilateral Malabar 2007 exercise held among the US, India, Japan, Australia, and Singapore in the

Bay of Bengal has raised China's concerns about the security of its sea lines of communication (SLOCs) in the IOR. In addition, the 2004 Indian Ocean earthquake and tsunami, which caused significant casualties and property loss, made China pay more attention to the Humanitarian Assistance and Disaster Relief (HADR) operations. It is in this background that China's maritime security strategy in the IOR region has evolved into a new phase.

During the period between November 1985 and January 1986, the PLA Navy first time sent its fleet consisting one destroyer and one replenishment ship abroad for friendly visit missions in the last 36 years since its independence in 1949. Chinese naval fleet visited Pakistan, Sri Lanka and Bangladesh three countries, making it remarkable for China's first time physical naval presence in the Indian Ocean region. During this period, China had dispatched several warships successively in the years of 1993, 2000, 2001, 2002, 2005 and 2007 to enter into the IOR for ocean-going training, friendly port calls and bilateral and multilateral naval exercise with states in this region. Among them, the most remarkable event should be the first global voyage conducted by a PLA naval formation including one destroyer and one comprehensive replenishment ship. The naval fleet visited ten countries around the world, spanning the Pacific Ocean, the Indian Ocean and the Atlantic Ocean, fourteen major straits and Suez and Panama Canals, lasting for more than four months with a total voyage of more than 33,000 nautical miles (Mei and Liu 2017). It has created the record of the longest sailing time, the largest number of visited countries and the farthest voyage in the history of PLA Navy. In 2005, the PLA Navy had conducted joint search and rescue exercises with Pakistan and India successively in the North Indian Ocean. Two years earlier, China had conducted similar exercises with Pakistan and India in the East China Sea off Shanghai. In 2007, Chinese Navy first time dispatched its destroyer Guangzhou to participate in the multinational maritime exercise 'AMAN-07' in the Arabian Sea. In addition to naval increasing presence in the IOR, Chinese companies also played an active role in the infrastructure construction activities such as highway, railway, port, and airport, etc. However, China's economic activities were described by some western countries as the 'string of pearls' strategy through which China can exercise its influence in the IOR.

Phase III (between 2009 and till date)

This period witnessed the shift of China's navy strategy from 'offshore waters defense' to the combination of 'offshore waters defense' with 'open seas protection' and its continuous and even permanent military presence in the IOR (The State Council Information Office 2015). The reasons contributed to this shift mainly lie in the expansion of China's overseas interests in terms of political, economic and strategic aspects, and also the increasing security challenges in both traditional and non-traditional security areas.

After a long period of rapid development, China has emerged as the second largest economy in 2010, largest exporter in 2009, and the largest oil importer in 2018. According to one report from World Trade Organization on international trade statistics in 2015, as a result of joining the WTO, China surpassed Japan as the leading Asian exporter, and overtook the US and Germany in 2007 and 2009 respectively to become the world's leading exporter (WTO 2015). In 2013, Chinese government launched the initiatives of 'The Silk Road Economic Belt' and '21st Century Maritime Silk Road', which are called China's Belt and Road Initiative (BRI). However, Chinese overseas interests are facing challenges ranging from struggles among major powers, regional turmoil, piracy, maritime terrorism, natural disasters, climate change, smuggle, and overfishing, etc. The most remarkable event for China's maritime security operation in this period should be its anti-piracy operations in the Gulf of Aden.

By the end of 2018, the PLA Navy has dispatched 31 naval contingents, 100 warships, 67 ship-borne helicopters, more than 26,000 officers and sailors to carry out 1,198 batches of escort missions, safely escorted more than 6,600 Chinese and foreign vessels, successfully rescued, received and rescued more than 70 Chinese and foreign vessels, and arrested 3 pirates (Chen and Li 2018: 1). With the regular deployment of Chinese escort task forces in the Gulf of Aden for anti-piracy missions, PLA Naval warships achieved normalization for regular supply through foreign ports. The regular replenishment network includes ports such as Port of Aden (Yemen), Salalah Port (Oman), Djibouti Port (Djibouti), and Jeddah Port (Saudi Arabia) four ports. In addition, Chinese naval taskforces sometimes also make technical stops at several ports in the Indian Ocean and beyond for refueling and restocking. These ports include Port of Colombo (Sri Lanka), Port of Karachi (Pakistan), Port of Changi (Singapore), Port Klang (Malaysia), and Port Victoria (Seychelles), etc.

China has also cooperated with the Combined Task Force (CTF) 151, CTF 465, and other states such as Russia, India, South Korea. The PLA Navy also make long post-anti-piracy travels to other states for friendly visits, bilateral or multilateral exercises, evacuation operations, HADR, and naval ceremonies, etc. For example, by the end 2018, Chinese anti-piracy task forces have carried out 103 visit missions to 63 countries and regions (Chen and Li 2018). China's naval presence in the Gulf of Aden operations also provided China to test its naval operations, when some warships which involved in this region were sent to the war-torn West Asia-North Africa (WANA) to evacuate Chinese citizens from Libya in 2011 and Yemen in 2015. In addition, China's warships also participated in the HADR operations such as MH370 search and rescue operation.

In addition to PLA Naval anti-piracy operations in the Gulf of Aden, China's maritime security strategy also include establishment of its first overseas military base, infrastructure construction and naval arms transfers, etc. According to Srikanth Kondapalli, one of India's leading academic analysts on the PLA,

> China is to influence substantially the structure of maritime power in the IOR through semi-military alliances, dual-use port facilities, stationing of non-combat troops initially abroad, MOOTW missions and arms transfers to the region. (Kondapalli 2018: 119)

Sino-Indian Maritime Security Cooperation in the Indian Ocean Region

Sino-Indian maritime security cooperation includes official visits, ship visits, joint maritime drills and exercises, anti-piracy cooperation, and maritime affairs dialogue, etc.

Official Visits

Since the end of the Cold War, the relations between China and India have improved a lot. Against this backdrop, China and India have exchanged frequently between defence ministers and other high officials in the maritime security field. Indian Defence Ministers visited China in July 1992, April 2003, May 2006, July 2013, and April 2016; while Chinese counterparts visited Indian in September 1994, September 2012, and August 2018. Indian high naval officials including Chiefs of Naval Staff, Vice Chiefs of Naval Staff paid friendly visits to China in March 1996, April 2005, April 2009, April 2010, and April 2014, while China counterparts paid visits to India in October 2005, November 2008.

Ship Visits

The friendly exchanges between the Chinese and Indian navies date back to the golden age of relations between the two countries in the 1950s. In 1956, during Chinese former Premier Zhou Enlai's visit to India, he visited an Indian warship in Mumbai Port and had lunch with Indian Navy officers and soldiers on board. In 1958, the Indian Navy sent one warship, called Indian Naval Ship (INS) Mysore, visited Shanghai, Nanjing and Hongkong (enroute), China, marking the first such naval visit since Indian Independence. Sino-Indian military exchanges have been interrupted after the 1962 border conflict and did not recover until the 1990s.

In the early 1994, the PLA Navy first time sent its training ship Zheng He to visit Mumbai, India. In October 1995, two Indian Naval ships visited Shanghai, China after participation in Indonesian Fleet Review (IFR) in Jakarta to celebrate 50th Anniversary of Indonesian Independence, which was the first port call to China for Indian naval ships after 37 years since 1958.

In September 2000, on the occasion of the 50th anniversary of the establishment of diplomatic ties between China and India, the Indian warships, INS Delhi and INS Kora, paid a 4-day goodwill visit to Shanghai, which marked the third time in independent India's history for Indian warship(s) to visit China. In May 2001, the PLA Naval fleet including one destroyer Harbin and one replenishment ship Taicang visited Mumbai. As visiting foreign ships, Chinese Naval ships were first time allowed to dock at naval port of Indian Western Fleet (Zhang 2003).

In November 2003, Indian Eastern Fleet including one guided missile destroyer INS Ranjit, one guided missile corvette INS Kulish and one replenishment tanker INS Jyoti visited Shanghai to conduct joint search and rescue exercise with PLA Navy. Indian Navy was welcomed by over 30 ships and submarines from the PLA Navy side. In 2005, the PLA Naval fleet including one destroyer Shenzhen and one comprehensive replenishment ship Weishanhu visited Indian port Kochito conduct joint maritime search and rescue exercise with Indian Navy. In April 2007, Indian Naval fleet including destroyer Rana and destroyer Ranjit arrived in Qingdao, China and started a 4-day visit.

In April 2009, Indian Naval fleet including INS Mumbai, INS Ranvir, INS Khanjar and INS Jyoti was invited by China to participate in its IFR in Qingdao for 60th anniversary of the establishment of the PLA Navy. In August 2009, one PLA Naval destroyer Shenzhen made port call at the Kochi port. In May 2012, PLA Naval training ship Zheng He visited Kochi. In June 2012, Indian Naval fleet including INS Rana, INS Shivalik, INS Karmuk and INS Shakti paid a port call to Shanghai. In August 2013, PLA Naval hospital ship Peace Ark paid a 6-day visit to Mumbai. In April 2014, the Indian Navy's stealth frigate, INS Shivalik, was invited by China for the multilateral maritime exercise under the framework of Western Pacific Naval Symposium at Qingdao. It is reported that during this visit, Indian warship captain refused Chinese former PLA Navy Admiral Wu Shengli's request to view Combat Information Centre of this frigate (Boehler 2014). In May 2014, the PLA Naval fleet including Zheng He and frigate Weifang first time visited Visakhapatnam headquarter of the Indian Eastern Fleet.

During the four years between 2014 and 2018, the Indian Naval warships have not visited China, while the PLA Naval ships visited India twice in 2015 and 2016 respectively. In April 2015, PLA Naval destroyer Ji'nan paid a 4-day visit to Mumbai. In February 2016, PLA Naval fleet including two frigates, Liuzhou and Sanya, participated in Indian IFR in Visakhapatnam, India. In 2017, PLA Navy proposed a port call by three warships including a destroyer, a frigate and a replenishment ship to Kochi between 4 and 7 June 2017. However, PLA Navy received the permission too late and had to cancel the trip. Chinese officials suggested that the delay was tantamount to a 'denial', while the Indian side disagreed with China's claim that its proposal has been denied, conceded that 'concerns within New Delhi's strategic establishment had delayed a decision' (Kasturi 2017). This issue reflects the tensions between China and India on the BRI. Since PLA Naval ships were taking closely maps the maritime component of the BRI, India was afraid of allowing PLA Navy warships to dock at Kochi will give the impression of Indian endorsement of Chinese Belt and Road Initiative. As a part of BRI, many Indian scholars believe that BRI will 'strengthen Beijing's strategic influence in South Asia' (Kasturi 2017). And Indian government also criticized China-Pakistan Economic Corridor (CPEC) project ignores Indian core concerns about sovereignty and territorial integrity.

Joint Maritime Drills and Exercises

With the gradual improvement of bilateral relationship between China and India since 1990s, the Indian military had a long desire to contact Chinese counterparts. In 1992, when his visit to China, Indian former Defence Minister Sharad Pawar proposed that China and India should carry out joint naval drills (Tang 2003a). According to the weekly magazine *India Today*, in February 2001, India had invited 26 countries and 70 warships including the US and Chinese navies to participate in its IFR exercise in the waters near Mumbai. China, however, declined Indian invitation given 'the lack of good-neighborly and friendly relations', 'China's cautious attitude toward joining joint military exercises', and 'China's taking into consideration about the feeling of Pakistan' (Qian 2003).

On 15 September 2000, the two navies conducted what could be termed as the first joint exercise but that was 'only an exchange of personnel and basic manoeuvres, which lasted for about eight hours' and was a 'great success' (Joseph 2003).

On 14 November 2003, during Indian Eastern Fleet's visit to Shanghai, the PLA Navy and the Indian Navy conducted their first search and rescue exercise off the Shanghai coast in their bilateral relations with code name of 'Dolphin 0310', which marked a 'historic jump in defence relations' between China and India (Joseph 2003). The joint exercise involved preliminary search and rescue manoeuvres. The idea of joint military exercise was first proposed by India in April 2003 during the visit of Indian former Defence Minister George Fernandes to China. It was during former Prime Minister Atal Bihari Vajpayee's visit to China in June 2003 that the decision of the joint exercise was taken. However, there were obvious differences between China and India in terms of the content of the exercise. India proposed an anti-piracy exercise in the Strait of Malacca in accordance with the Indo-Indonesian or Indo-US naval military exercises, while China suggested that the anti-piracy operations should be carried out by the coastal defence vessels rather than naval warships. Therefore, China proposes that two countries hold search and rescue drills. After many consultations, New Delhi finally accepted Beijing's proposal (Tang 2003a). Furthermore, the location of the exercise was initially rumored to be in the Indian Ocean or East Coast of India (Tang 2003b). At last, the location turned out to be in the East China Sea off Shanghai.

In December 2005, China and India conducted their second joint search and rescue exercise in the northern Indian Ocean region. With the code of 'China-India Friendship 2005', this exercise lasted for nearly 4 hours. Chinese side was presented by two warships including destroyer Shenzhen and comprehensive replenishment ship Weishan Hu, while Indian side was presented by one frigate and one offshore patrol ship. The exercise included joint fleet formation and maritime joint search and rescue two courses. China and India conducted exercise such as communication, maneuvering, sea and air search, fleet replenishment, and joint rescue of damaged ships. It was the second time for Chinese and Indian navies to carry out non-traditional exercise and also the first time for PLA Navy to conduct exercise in the Indian Ocean region with Indian Navy.

On 16 April 2007, Chinese naval fleet and visiting Indian naval fleet conducted a joint maritime drill in the Yellow Sea off Qingdao. More than 1,000 officers and sailors participated in this lasting nearly 3-hour drill, and practiced the courses such as lighting communication, semaphore exchange and formation transformation, etc.

On 23 April 2009, the Indian Chief of Naval Staff attended the International Fleet Review 2009 at Qingdao for 60th anniversary of the founding of the PLA Navy. In addition to Chinese 25 vessels and 31 aircraft, a total number of 14 countries including India and 21 vessels also participated in this IFR. These participating countries included Russia, the US, France, Pakistan, South Korea, Australia, New Zealand, Singapore, Thailand, Bangladesh, Brazil, Canada and Mexico (Liu 2019).

During 4–8 February 2016, the PLA Naval fleet including three warships was invited to attend the Indian IFR 2016 at Vishakhapatnam port. IFR 2016 was the second international review hosted and conducted by the Indian Navy, and it also was the first time for the PLA Navy to participate in Indian IFR. The IFR 2016 was culminated with the Passage Exercise (PASSEX) undertaken by Indian and foreign Naval ships in the Bay of Bengal on 9 February 2016. The exercise witnessed participation by 34 Indian Naval ships and 20 foreign warships from 14 countries, aimed at 'fostering greater cooperation and camaraderie with friendly foreign navies, increasing interoperability, providing the requisite operational element' (Press Information Bureau 2016).

In 2014, the Indian Navy was invited to attend China's IFR and multilateral maritime exercise at Qingdao held by the PLA Navy to commemorate its 65th anniversary of founding. The IFR, however, was cancelled on 15 April by China due to 'the special situation and atmosphere surrounding the continuing search for the missing Malaysian airliner MH 370' (Pang 2014). On 23 April 2014, Indian Navy participated in the multinational maritime exercise 'Sea Cooperation-2014' along with other 6 foreign navies from Pakistan, Indonesia, Singapore, Malaysia, Bangladesh, and Brunei. With the theme of joint search and rescue at sea, this exercise mainly conducted six subject exercises, including formation communication, formation movement, replenishment at sea, joint rescue, joint anti-hijacking, and light weapons shooting, with the aim of 'enhancing understanding, consensus, mutual trust and friendship with the navies of various countries, discussing the organization and implementation of naval maritime joint search and rescue in various countries, and promoting pragmatic exchanges and cooperation between navies in maintaining maritime security' (Fu and Li 2014).

In addition to exercises mentioned above, both the PLA Navy and Indian Navy also take part in other multilateral maritime exercises led by other countries, such as Western Pacific Naval Symposium (WPNS) Multilateral Joint Maritime Exercise (in 2007), Rim of the Pacific Exercise (in 2014 and 2016), KOMODO Multilateral Humanitarian Assistance and Disaster Relief exercise (in 2014, 2016 and 2018), ASEAN Defence Ministers' Meeting (ADMM) Plus Exercise on Maritime Security and Counter Terrorism (in 2016), Indian Ocean Naval Symposium (IONS) Multilateral Search and Rescue Exercise (in 2017), Singapore IFR (in 2017), ASEAN IFR (in 2017), etc. However, it seems that Chinese and Indian Navies do not have close engagements in such multinational exercises.

Anti-piracy Cooperation

In 1996, China and India signed an agreement on joint efforts to combat piracy and gun smuggling (Wang 2009: 53).In 2004, 16 Asian governments including the 10 ASEAN countries, China, India, Japan, South Korea, Bangladesh and Sri Lanka signed the *Regional Cooperation Agreement on Combating Piracy and Armed Robbery against Ships in Asia*, (ReCAAP). In November 2006, according to the ReCAAP, the Information Sharing Centre was founded. The Center obtains intelligence on piracy through the Focal Points of individual member states, compiling and exchanging information on piracy and armed robbery at sea in Asia.

After the end of 2008, both China and India sent their warships to the Gulf of Aden for anti-piracy patrols due to the rising threats from pirates. Since January 2012, China and India have strengthened coordination with other states including Japan on convoy coordination. As China's white paper *The Diversified Employment of China's Armed Force* stated, they have adjusted their escort schedules on a quarterly basis, optimized available assets, and thereby enhanced escort efficiency. China, as the reference country for the first round of convoy coordination, submitted its escort timetable for the first quarter of 2012 in good time. India and Japan's escort task forces adjusted their convoy arrangements accordingly, thereby formulating a well-scheduled escort timetable (Information Office of the State Council 2013).

Maritime Affairs Dialogue

In March 2012, the Foreign Ministers between China and India first time decided to initiate the maritime affairs dialogue. During Chinese former Foreign Minister Yang Jiechi's visit to India in February and March 2012, both China and India agreed to carry out maritime security cooperation. India's External Affairs Ministry spokesman Syed Akbaruddin said, India and China will establish a maritime affairs dialogue, and it is expected to be led by the Indian Ministry of External Affairs (MEA) and the Chinese Ministry of Foreign Affairs. In September 2014, Chinese President Xi Jinping paid a state visit to India. According to the *Joint Statement*, China and India 'decided to hold the first round of maritime cooperation dialogue within this year to exchange views on maritime affairs and security, including anti-piracy, freedom of navigation and cooperation between maritime agencies of both countries' (MEA 2014).

On 4 February 2016, China and India held the inaugural China-India Maritime Affairs Dialogue in New Delhi. Kong Xuanyou, Assistant Minister of the Ministry of Foreign Affairs of China and Amandeep Singh Gill, Joint Secretary in the MEA co-chaired the dialogue. The dialogue covered issues of mutual interest, including 'exchange of perspectives on maritime security, developments in international regimes such as UNCLOS and IMO and prospects for maritime cooperation' (MEA 2016). Beijing said the next round China-India Maritime Affairs Dialogue will be held in Beijing on a mutually convenient date in 2017 (Qin and Chang 2016). Although the first dialogue was essentially an 'ice-breaker' amid the Sino-Indian tensions in the Indian Ocean and South China Sea, it contributes the trust between China and India and strengthens cooperation in maritime security field (Khurana 2016).

On 13 July 2018, China and India held the second Maritime Affairs Dialogue in Beijing after one year and a half. According to the press release of MEA, the two sides exchanged views on various topics of mutual interest, including perspectives on 'maritime security and cooperation, blue economy, and further strengthening of practical cooperation', and Indian side also elaborated its vision for the Indo-Pacific (MEA 2018). According to China's side, the two sides have exchanged in-depth views on maritime development strategies, maritime security situation and Sino-Indian maritime cooperation (Ministry of Foreign Affairs 2018).

In addition to Maritime Affairs Dialogue, China and India also involved in the engagement in the multilateral maritime security management mechanism, such as the Indian Ocean Rim Association (IORA), the Indian Ocean Naval Symposium and the South Asian Association for Regional Cooperation (SAARC), etc.

Sino-Indian Maritime Security Relations

As noted, Sino-Indian maritime security cooperation has several characteristics as follows. Firstly, Sino-Indian maritime security cooperation started late and developed slowly. The Sino-Indian maritime security cooperation began in the year of 2000 and was slow to develop, even though India proposed to China the idea of maritime security cooperation in the early 1990s since the end of Cold War. Secondly, Shino-Indian maritime security cooperation has remained at a low level, both in terms of scope and depth. The Sino-Indian maritime security cooperation mainly focuses on low-sensitivity non-traditional security fields such as warship exchanges, joint search and rescue exercises, and anti-piracy cooperation, and almost does not involve traditional security fields. Finally, Sino-Indian maritime security cooperation has not achieved much substantive results, more like a barometer and symbol of their bilateral relations. In addition, Sino-Indian maritime security activities have not been institutionalized and are easily interrupted, postponed and even cancelled due to the impact of bilateral relations and external factors. For example, the Indian Navy and the Chinese Navy have not yet established regular joint exercises, just as India did with other permanent members of the UN Security Council, such as the Malabar exercise with the US, Indra exercise with Russia, Konkan exercise with Britain and Varuna with France.

The main reason for this lies in the lack of mutual trust between China and India. On one hand, factors such as unresolved border dispute, historical memory of border conflict in 1962, anti-terrorism issue, and trade imbalance, etc can influence Sino-Indian maritime security cooperation. On the other hand, both China and India misunderstand each other's maritime security strategy/activity in the IOR. With the increasing dependent on the security of SLOCs in the IOR in terms of energy and trade, China concerns about India's desire to dominate the Indian Ocean region, and its closer engagement with major extra-regional powers, especially with the US and Japan. Likewise, India is also afraid of the potential threats and challenges to its national security posed by Chinese maritime security strategy and activities in the IOR. India is suspicious that China is trying to encircle India through a series of diplomatic, economic and military steps. Firstly, India concerns about China's close diplomatic relations with states along its neighbours, such as Pakistan and Bangladesh. The former is viewed as

China's 'all-weather ally'. Secondly, India keeps an eye on Chinese economic activities in this region, such as Maritime Silk Road (MSR) initiative, one part of the Belt and Road Initiative. Most debates on China's economic activity focus on the violation of India's territorial sovereignty and integrity, lack of transparency, imbalanced benefit distribution between China and host countries, debt trap, and potential military use to threat Indian national security, etc. Thirdly, in the military aspect, India is worried about China's rising naval presence in the IOR, such as sending submarines for anti-piracy operations, submarine port calls to Sri Lanka and Pakistan, China's first overseas military base in Djibouti, and arms transfer to Indian neighbouring countries, etc. In addition, given the trust deficit between China and India, it seems that both of them don't feel imperative and urgent to take joint action to enhance maritime security, because they can achieve their maritime security goals through self-help and cooperation with other states, although they are facing common threats from a series of non-traditional threats, such as piracy, maritime terrorism and natural disasters, etc.

There is no doubt that China experienced growing and rising presence in the Indian Ocean Region. Most scholars believe that there is Sino-Indian competition for naval dominance or security dilemma in the Indian Ocean region. For the long-term stability and prosperity, both China and India should engage with each other. Firstly, both China and India should narrow and remove their exaggerated threat perceptions on each other's maritime security strategy/activity in the IOR. China has neither intention nor the capability to encircle India in the IOR; Likewise, India has no capability to dominate the Indian Ocean. As emerging powers with nuclear weapons, both China and Indian live in the dynamic world characterized by interdependence and mutual deterrence. Secondly, China and India should promote their maritime security ranging from non-traditional security to traditional security fields, from less-sensitive to high-sensitive cooperation. Thirdly, given the loose nature of the maritime security cooperation in the IOR, China and India should try to strengthen their maritime cooperation in the multilateral platforms to contribute to the maritime security in the Indian Ocean and beyond.

References

Boehler, Patrick. 2014. 'Indian Warship Captain Refuses Chinese Admiral's Request to View Command Centre', *South China Morning Post*, https://www.scmp.com/news/china-insider/article/1496586/indian-warship-captain-refuses-chinese-admirals-request-view (accessed on 23 April 2019).

Chen, Guoquan and Li, Tang. 2018. '护航10年，中国海军亚丁湾上奏响平安乐章' [Escort for Ten Years, the Chinese Navy Plays a Peaceful Chapter on the Gulf of Aden], *Ministry of Defense, People's Republic of China*, http://www.mod.gov.cn/action/2018-12/27/content_4832952.htm (accessed on 24 April 2019).

Cottrell, A. J. and Burrell, B. M. 1972.*The Indian Ocean: It's Political, Economic, and Military Importance.* Translated by Chinese scholars collectively, Shanghai: Shanghai People's Publishing House.

Fu, Long and Li, Qi.2014 '图解"海上合作-2014"多国海上联合演习参演舰艇' [Picture Showing the Warships Participating in the "Maritime Cooperation - 2014" Multinational Maritime Joint Exercise], *Renmin Wang*, http://military.people.com.cn/n/2014/0423/c1011-24934387.html (accessed on 11 March 2019).

Information Office of the State Council. 2013. *The Diversified Employment of China's Armed Forces*, People's Republic of China, http://www.scio.gov.cn/zfbps/ndhf/2013/Document/1312843/1312843.htm (accessed on 23 April 2019).

Joseph, Josy. 2003. 'Indian, Chinese Naval Ships Engage in Joint Exercise off Shanghai', *Rediff India Abroad*, www.rediff.com/news/2003/nov/15navy.htm (accessed on 23 April 2019).

Kasturi, Charu Sudan. 2017. 'Chinese Navy Hits India Wall', *The Telegraph*, https://www.telegraphindia.com/india/chinese-navy-hits-india-wall/cid/1500559 (accessed on 23 April 2019).

Khurana, Gurpreet S.2016. 'First China-India Maritime Dialogue: Beyond 'Icebreaking'', *National Maritime Foundation*, http://www.maritimeindia.org/View%20Profile/635917882555223208.pdf (accessed on 23 Apirl 2019).

Kondapalli, Srikanth. 2018. 'China's Evolving Naval Presence in the Indian Ocean Region: An Indian Perspective', in David Brewster (ed.), *India*

& China at Sea: Competition for Naval Dominance in the Indian Ocean, pp. 111-24, New Delhi: Oxford University Press.

Liu, Xuan. 2019. '中国将举行海军成立70周年多国海军活动或为阅舰式' [China Will Hold a Multinational Naval Event for the 70th Anniversary of the Navy's Establishment or for the Fleet Review], *Uschinapress*, http://www.uschinapress.com/2019/0228/1157401.shtml (accessed on 11 March 2019).

MEA. 2014. *Joint Statement between the Republic of India and the People's Republic of China on Building a Closer Developmental Partnership*, Government of India, https://www.mea.gov.in/bilateral-documents.htm?dtl/24022/Joint_Statement_between_the_Republic_of_India_and_the_Peoples_Republic_of_China_on_Building_a_Closer_Developmental_Partnership (accessed on 15 March 2019).

MEA. 2018. 'Second India-China Maritime Affairs Dialogue', *Government of India*, https://www.mea.gov.in/press-releases.htm?dtl/30048/Second_IndiaChina_Maritime_Affairs_Dialogue (accessed on 15 April 2019).

Mei, Shixiong and Liu, Changbao. 2017. '第一次环球航行：总航程3.3万海里' [First Global Voyage: Total Voyage Distance of 33,000 Nautical Miles], *Xinhuanet*, http://www.xinhuanet.com//politics/2017-08/16/c_1121493337.htm (accessed on 24 April 2019).

Ministry of External Affairs. 2016. 'Inaugural India-China Maritime Affairs Dialogue', *Government of India4 February 2016*, http://mea.gov.in/press-releases.htm?dtl/26317/Inaugural+IndiaChina+Maritime+Affairs+Dialogue (accessed on 15 March 2019).

Ministry of Foreign Affairs. 2018. '中印举行第二轮海上合作对话' [China and Indian Conducted Second Round of Maritime Cooperation], *People's Republic of China*, https://www.fmprc.gov.cn/web/wjbxw_673019/t1577052.shtml (accessed on 15 March 2019).

Pang, Qi. 2014. 'Chinese Navy Marks 65th Anniversary with International Drills in Qingdao', *Global Times*, http://www.globaltimes.cn/content/855837.shtml (accessed on 11 March 2019).

Press Information Bureau. 2016. 'IFR 2016 - Passage Exercise - AU Revoir till we Meet Again', *Ministry of Defence, Government of India*, http://pib.nic.in/newsite/PrintRelease.aspx?relid=136280 (accessed on 11 March 2019).

Qian, Feng. 2003. '主动倡议加强接触，印度想和中国搞联合军演' [Initiative to Strengthen Contacts, India Wants to Engage in Joint Forces with China], Renmin Wang, http://www.people.com.cn/GB/junshi/2139065.html (accessed on 23 April).

Qin, Boya and Chang, Hong. 2016. '中印举行首轮海上合作对话' [China and India Conducted First Round of Maritime Cooperation Dialogue], Renmin Wang, http://world.people.com.cn/n1/2016/0205/c1002-28113506.html (accessed on 23 April 2019).

Tang, Lu. 2003a. '印度1992年曾建议中印联合演练，今年4月最终敲定' [India Proposed a Sino-Indian Joint Exercise in 1992 and Finalized It in April This Year], *China News*, http://www.chinanews.com/n/2003-1114/26/368812.html 2/2 (accessed 23 April 2019).

Tang, Lu. 2003b. '中印首次海军联合军事演习' [First Sino-Indian Naval Joint Military Exercise], *Eastday*, http://tj.eastday.com/epublish/gb/paper532/30/class053200002/hwz1329651.htm (accessed on 23 April 2019).

The State Council Information Office. 2015. *China's Military Strategy*, People's Republic of China, http://www.scio.gov.cn/zfbps/ndhf/2015/Document/1435159/1435159.htm (accessed on 24 April 2019).

Wang, Lirong. 2009. '印度洋与中国海上通道安全战略' [The Indian Ocean and the Chinese Strategy for Maritime Security], *South Asian Studies*, (3): 46-54.

WTO. 2015. *International Trade Statistics 2015*, World Trade Organization, https://www.wto.org/english/res_e/statis_e/its2015_e/its2015_e.pdf (accessed on 23 April 2019).

Zhang, Aijing. 2003. '中印海军将首次联合军演，印三大主力舰昨天抵上海' [Chinese and Indian Navies Will Conduct First Joint Military Exercises, and Three Indian Naval Main Warships Arrived in Shanghai Yesterday], *Renmin Wang*, http://www.people.com.cn/GB/junshi/1076/2180473.html (accessed on 23 April 2019).

List of Abbreviations

ADMM	ASEAN Defence Ministers' Meeting
BRI	Belt and Road Initiative
CTF	Combined Task Force
CPEC	China-Pakistan Economic Corridor
HADR	Humanitarian Assistance and Disaster Relief
IFR	Indonesian Fleet Review
INS	Indian Naval Ship
IONS	Indian Ocean Naval Symposium
IOR	Indian Ocean Region
IORA	Indian Ocean Rim Association
MEA	Ministry of External Affairs
MSR	Maritime Silk Road
PASSEX	Passage Exercise
PLA	People's Liberation Army
ReCAAP	Regional Cooperation Agreement on Combating Piracy and Armed Robbery against Ships in Asia
SARRC	South Asian Association for Regional Cooperation
SLOCs	Sea Lines of Communication
US	the United States
WANA	West Asia-North Africa
WTO	World Trade Organization
WPNS	Western Pacific Naval Symposium

Emerging Trends on Security and Threats to China's Maritime Domain: A Maritime Security Framework Approach

Ramnath Reghunadhan

Introduction

The concept and contextualisation of maritime security is said to have begun in the Pre-historic times by the Egyptians, who is believed to have built the first "war-canoes" in 5500 BCE, on which many art forms in caves and on rocks emerged (Figure 1). It is considered to be one of the earliest instances where recorded the oldest form of naval warfare of the human civilisation is said to have taken place. The conflict over the maritime domain between human would have happened thousands of years preceding that, especially when primitive forms of boats or "rafts" made of "papyrus seeds" have been in use. But, the securitization of maritime domain (atleast in modern conception) has only developed with the development and use of war-canoes in and around Northern Africa and later on towards the rest of the world. This also led to the development of ship-building technologies, ancient articulation of maritime operations, and the delineation of maritime domain into "home waters" and/or "foreign waters," along with the origin of maritime forces (Gilbert, 2008). Figure 1 shows an art of a pre-historic period war-canoe in Egypt.

Figure 1: An Art of a Prehistoric Period war-canoe in Egypt

Prehistoric war-canoe

Source: Gilbert, 2008: p. 8.

Later on various civilizations and nations developed their own capabilities and forces in relation to large water bodies. This later initiated the large-scale use of oceans and seas, one which led to the contextualization, what is now considered as the maritime domain. Historically, all major 'Great Powers' have depended on the maritime domain to extend (not just) the commercial facets like trade and capital, but have engaged in militarisation and in 'show of force' as well (Sparks, 1997). The strength in the maritime domain entails as well as ensures provision and opportunity of greater leverage for State actors, which at least have been the prime focus in the modern times. In addition, all of these actors enabled security-induced maritime defence mechanisms, which was (and still is) linked to their national interest and sovereignty, an idea to which China is no different.

Maritime security and strategy is an inherent part of China's aspirations to be a global power, one which it takes very seriously. Once, the French Emperor Napoleon Bonaparte (1769-1821) during the peak of military conquests to establish an empire believed that China is a sleeping giant with immense potential to control the world, which exclusively included the seas. He said, "Let China sleep, for when she wakes she will shake the world" (Fish 2016). The American naval strategist, historian and theoretical analyst of the name Alfred Thayer Mahan once opined on how that it will be "difficult to contemplate with equanimity such a vast mass... [with] millions [of Chinese population]... concentrated into one effective political organization, equipped with modern appliances, and cooped within a territory already narrow for it" (Sempa, 2014). The paper looks at the emergence and related complexity of security, warfare and its impact and implications on China's maritime domain, providing an overview through the maritime security framework approach, the threats and incidents there forth in the maritime domain. To deal with this, not only requires new technological, tactical and strategic offensive and defensive capabilities and apparatus, especially from China, India needs to look at various strategic options as well.

Methodology

A framework analysis have been undertaken to induce the possibilities for maritime organizations to reduce vulnerabilities to targeted attacks and threats from rivals and enemies. An extensive review of literature, content analysis of reports and documents by governments, international organizations and related analysis have been undertaken. In the maritime security framework approach, the matrix encompassing operationalization of concepts include blue water navy, maritime economy, maritime safety and finally analyzing security in the context of capabilities and threats of China in the maritime domain.

China

In his book *The Problem of Asia and its Effect upon International Policies (1900)*, besides correctly predicting the rise of Cold War, Mahan also recognized the "immense latent force" of China, and its subsequent rise. In the very first chapter of *The Influence of Sea Power upon History (1660-1783)*, Mahan describes sea or ocean as "great highway," which had "strategic chokepoints" which comprises of the modern sea lanes of communication (SLOC). Interestingly, a scholar who dominated both academic and military domains from the beginning of the end of latter half of 19th century, writing voluminous amounts of literature on sea power, national security, balance of power and history Mahan was to a great extent emphasized the rise of China rivalling all other major powers of his time. His understanding of the "anarchical nature of international politics" and the related world system has rightly positioned China in the currently emerging transitional but disruptive world stage. Mahan interpreted "sea power," viz. e. viz. maritime security as the most important aspect of power and sustenance of any aspiring power. This stands posited as all powers compete to become Blue Water Navy like the British Empire in the 19th century and the US in the 20th century (Sempa, 2014).

Historically, China has been a seafaring 'civilization', with the interlinkages of trade and people-to-people exchange later came to known to have been part of the famous 'Silk Road'. In terms of naval warfare capabilities and militarization, it was in 7th century B.C, during the period of Chou dynasty that development in that respect were seen. Moreover, this is the same period in which Sun Tzu wrote and completed his work, *The Art of War*, emphasizing on "rational planning, flexible methods and efficient use of resources." This is because of the requirements to protect China's trade and security interests, as well as increased need to procure tributes from other nations as well (Kane, p. 18). In the 21st century, China has 'woken up' as a power capable of 'shaking' the world, and does not seem to be stopped or ignored by any country in the world. More importantly, for the past few years China seemed to have initiated the process of reordering and restructuring the world order, one which entails increasing maritime capabilities. In international relations, maritime security is one of the key areas in the domain of national security. But unlike the powers that precede China, the world is more complex in the sense that its rival powers like USA, India and Japan have huge trade, economic and strategic interdependence with it. This complicates the issue and in turn initiates action-reaction mechanism, whereby any one of set of action by China leads to one or set of reaction by the other power and vice versa. The major linchpin of this type of system can be the huge set of cost, each nation-state have to face in terms of the impact on the economy, society and stability of the country, region and world as a whole. In a period of interconnectedness through digital and regional connectivity, this entails greater impact and destruction over any nation, irrespective of their power and wherewithal. In 2013, Chinese Communist Party's (CCP) Politburo started academic sessions and workshops to look into further projecting China as a "major maritime power" (Masuda, 2013). The maritime security framework approach entailed in this study encompasses the operationalization of various concepts and are given in the following sections.

Chinese Blue Water Navy: It goes without doubt that any country's intention to achieve blue water navy capability foresees possibilities to achieve efficient, effective and accomplished modernization of its naval and sea-based forces. It is critical for a country like China that looks at entailing further military preponderance in the region. Many have argued that China's necessity to achieve Blue Water Navy capability is related to its intention to either contest, resist or even surpass the US military wherewithal in the future. This particularly, at least in the present context focuses on countering US presence in Indo-Pacific, establish its eminence among allies and to achieve a "unified China" in the future. Scholars and military practitioners have argued that this will entail the emergence of the naval force as a hybrid. Dr Patrick Cronin, the Director of CNAS's (Centre for a New American Security) Asia-Pacific Security Programme was quoted saying that "By 2030, the existence of a global Chinese navy will be an important, influential and fundamental fact of international politics." This will further expand the intersectional ties with maximizing enemy force attrition, to deny attribution, plausible and critical chokepoints, sea lanes of communication (SLOC), reduce threats from piracy to trade, shipping ports as well as to improve global governance under Chinese leadership. Interestingly, by achieving the capability China could and will extend or project its capabilities to the extended neighborhood (Pharis, 2009; Bloomberg, 2017).

Based on recent estimates by Bloomberg, by the end of next decade Chinese naval forces are expected to overtake US in the category of attack submarines (double), ballistic missile submarines (just edging out) and small surface ships (three times) than that of the US naval forces. But US is expected to retain its dominance in large surface ships (almost three times) and in the number of aircraft carriers (three times) than that of China (Table 1). Table 1 provides a comparison as well as extrapolation between naval forces of China and USA from 2000 to 2016 and 2030, based on the provisional funds allocated by both the countries, and various vision and policy documents from both the countries.

Table 1: Comparison between naval forces of China and USA

Category	China			USA		
	2000	2016	2030 (est.)	2000	2016	2030 (est.)
Attack Submarines	64	56	87	55	57	42
Ballistic Missile Submarines	1	4	12	18	14	11
Small Surface Ships	79	103	123	62	23	40
Large Surface Ships	20	19	34	79	84	95
Aircraft Carriers	0	1	4	12	10	11
Total	163	183	260	226	188	199

Source: Bloomberg, 2017

Maritime economy: The Xi Administration is vehemently pursuing the policy of '21st Century Maritime Silk Road' that it looks for enhancing bilateral and multilateral cooperation among various State actors. It was during the period Chinese 'reform and opening' by Deng Xiaoping that the induction of the concept of China's maritime economy was first introduced as a parameter of measuring contributions to the Chinese economy. It was during the Meeting of National Planning Office of Philosophy and Social Science, the Chinese economists DixinXu and Guangyuan Yu introduced the concept of maritime economy among the indicators to measure economic contributions and growth. In 1980s, the estimated contribution was 4.7 billion USD, which later increased five-fold in the next decade. Interestingly, between '90s and the beginning of the 21st century, this increased ten-fold to 49.93 billion USD. Furthermore, the contributions of primary, secondary and tertiary sector steadily increases from 2002 to 2017, reaching a total contribution of 1.15 trillion USD (Figure 2).

Figure 2: China's Maritime Economy 2002-17

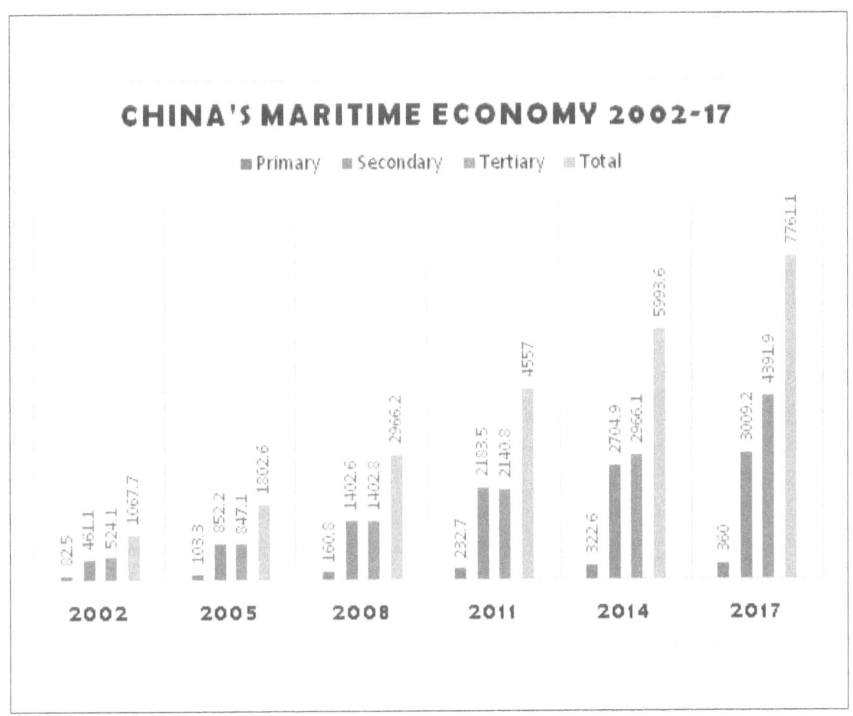

Source: To& Lee, 2018

Thus the gross productions value for the last five years increased by 7.5 per cent, accounting for about one-tenth of the country's total GDP. In 2013, the top ten contributions from coastal provinces came from Guangdong (20.78 per cent), Shandong (17.85 per cent), Shanghai (11.61 per cent), Zheijiang (9.68 per cent), Fujian (9.26 per cent), Jiangsu (9.06 per cent), Tianjin (8.38 per cent), Liaoning (6.89 per cent), Hebei (3.21 per cent), and Guangxi (1.66 per cent). Further, in 2017, the major contributors to China's maritime economy were coastal tourism (209.98 billion USD), maritime transportation (90.56 billion USD), marine fishery & aquaculture (67.09 billion USD), marine engineering architecture (26.41 billion USD), marine shipbuilding (20.88 billion USD), offshore oil and gas (16.15 billion USD) and marine chemicals (14.97 billion USD). The government plans to send "three maritime satellites" in improving maritime research, to entail further integration and cohesiveness in its activities to deal with ecological issues, marine pollution and research, including those by "icebreaker Xuelong and deep-sea manned submersible Jiaolong." China is further looking at options to establish "marine economy demonstration zones" and further "foster world-class high-end marine industrial clusters in Guangdong-Hong Kong-Macao Greater Bay Area, and build Shanghai and Shenzhen into global marine centers."(Sun et al., 2018; To and Lee, 2018; Liangyu, 2018).

Maritime Safety: In the mid-90s, when the International Maritime Organisation (IMO) amended the international treaty that entail on standardizing training and certification of sailors, China was among the first section of countries that submitted the requisite implementation reports (Xinhua, 2000).The nodal agency that ensues on maritime safety within the country is the China Maritime Safety Administration (China MSA) that implements the International Convention on Standards of Training, Certification and Watch keeping for Seafarers (1978), but was instituted in the year 2000. The China MSA is active in the coastline of the country as well as along the rivers Yangtze, Pearl and Heilongjiang. The major responsibilities include "maritime safety, security, prevention of pollution from ships, and protection of seafarers' rights." This agency comes as well as the China Rescue & Salvage (CRS) (the successor of People's Salvage Company) comes under the Ministry of Transport, while the Maritime Police comes under the Border Control Department (BCD). These agencies are focused on the civilian sector, while the defence agencies operate within their respective internal agencies under the People's Liberation Army Navy (PLAN). Besides, China has ratified nearly three dozen conventions and code of various international organizations like IMO, International Labor

Organisation (ILO) (*Global Security*, 2014; UNESCAP, 1998; CRSA, 2018, Xiao, 2000), which is enunciated in Table 2.

Table 2: Conventions and codes accepted for international safety standards

<table>
<tr><td>

Conventions/ Codes for International Safety Standards

- ➤ International Dangerous Goods (IMDG) Code of 1965;
- ➤ Load Lines Convention of 1966 (LL);
- ➤ International Tonnage Convention of 1969;
- ➤ International Convention for the Prevention of Pollution from Ships (1973), amended in 1978 (MARPOL);
- ➤ International Convention on Maritime Search and Rescue of 1979 (SAR Convention);
- ➤ International Convention for the Safety of Life at Sea of 1974, amended in 1998 (SOLAS);
- ➤ The International Convention on Standards of Training, Certification and Watchkeeping for Seafarers of 1978, amended in 1995 and 2010 (STCW);
- ➤ The Code for the Safe Carriage of Irradiated Nuclear Fuel, Plutonium and High-Level Radioactive Wastes in Flasks (INF Code) of 1993;
- ➤ International Maritime Solid Bulk Cargo (IMSBC) Code;
- ➤ International code for construction and equipment of ships carrying liquefied gases in bulk (IGC) Code;
- ➤ International Grain Code; International code for construction and equipment of ships carrying dangerous chemicals in bulk (IBC) Code;
- ➤ International Ship and Port Facility Security (ISPS) Code;
- ➤ International Safety Management (ISM) Code;
- ➤ International Code for Intact Stability (IS Code);
- ➤ Code of safe practices for ships carrying Timber Deck Cargo (TDC Code);

</td></tr>
</table>

> ➤ Casualty Investigation Code;
>
> ➤ Code of Safe Practice for Cargo Stowage and securing (CSS Code);
>
> ➤ Code for the safety of Special Purpose Ships (SPS Code);
>
> ➤ Code of safe practices for Offshore Supply Vessel (OSV Code);
>
> ➤ Mobile Offshore Drilling Unit code (MODU Code);
>
> ➤ High-Speed Craft code (HSC Code);
>
> ➤ International Life Saving Appliances Code (LSA Code);
>
> ➤ International Fire Safety System Code (FSS Code);
>
> ➤ Fire Test Procedure Code (FTP Code);
>
> ➤ Polar Code of 2017;
>
> ➤ Code of Safe Working Practices for Merchant Seafarers;
>
> ➤ Code of Conduct for the Merchant Navy.
>
> Sources: Compiled by the Author

The international cooperation with countries and China have been increasing, particularly in terms of joint military exercises in the maritime domain. China has also signed Memorandum of Understanding (MoU) with various countries and international agencies in Paris, Latin-America Agreement, Tokyo, Caribbean, Mediterranean, Indian Ocean and Abuja, and is looking to extend to other regions as well (Xiao, 2000; Bhattacharjee, 2019). Now the final puzzle to analyzing the matrix of maritime security framework approach is used to conceptualize on the emerging cyber threats to China's maritime domain and has been done in the following section.

Emerging Threats: The emerging future of Chinese warfare overtones depend on many aspects, particularly the cyber preparedness, strategic implications and perceived threats and vulnerabilities that are emerging. In 2015, the Xi administration enunciated on the cybersecurity strategy, where he enunciated on four principles, *viz. e. viz.* "respect for cyber sovereignty, peace and security, openness and cooperation, and good order" (Chuanying, 2016). China has enhanced its cyber war technologies and capabilities in an environment which is seeing an increasing confrontation with the US, including both politically and economically. Unlike the conventional warfare, China is undertaking an asymmetric, non-linear warfare (together called hybrid warfare), that inherently resides on the use of high-end technologies or core technologies. These increasing security and technology preparedness from China, is in a direction that tends to confront with major powers as well. But more importantly, the asymmetric warfare or hybrid warfare as being coined in recent years are increasingly providing for threats that engulf and increase complexity of the regional security architecture of Chinese maritime sovereignty (Deshpande, 2018).

The concept of hybrid warfare is increasingly being used to describe the "use of asymmetric and non-linear strategies" usually by "great powers" as well as weak states and even to a certain extent by non-State actors. The dominant use of the term hybrid warfare increased with the American and European strategic studies describing Russian operations in its successful use of warfare tactics. It implies the "strategies that mobilize a variety of state levers of power, producing a blend of conventional and nonconventional tactics aimed at keeping the use of force under the threshold of open war. The hybridization of domains of contemporary warfare and its conceptualization is currently in greater use among scholars of strategic studies and defence personnel, who mostly entail on its use by American and European security establishment and academia. There are but constant risks, disagreements and political conflicts that are inherently linked with the international politics, which often create serious implications as well. Besides the US, the major regional maritime power that have increased skirmishes, the countries like Japan and ASEAN countries are also party to conflict in the seas. But often, the existing frameworks are lacking in identifying the inherent convergences as well as divergences.

Implications for India

India, which has a history of long-term strategic conflict and diverging interests with China, began with the String of Pearls to the recent Maritime Strategies, but have been a keen observer. But, Chinese engagements since the early times have started to increasingly assert itself into the Indian Ocean region and among its neighbours as well. This increased economic and strategic relationships between China and various nations in the Indian Ocean and are shown in Figure 3.

Figure 3: Shows economic and strategic engagements of China in the Indian Ocean.

Country	Active Naval Vessels Manufactured/Co-Developed by China*	Big-Ticket Maritime Infrastructure under development by China	Chinese Investment Spending 2005 – 2017 (in $ bn)+	Status of Free Trade Agreement with China
Bangladesh	46	Chittagong Port	24.1	Biggest Trading Partner, Feasibility Study Started in 2016
Maldives	0	Ihavanddhippolhu Integrated Development (iHavan) Project	NA	Signed (2017)
Myanmar	17	Kyaukpyu Deep Water Port	7.4	ASEAN-China Free Trade Area (2010)
Pakistan	15	Gwadar Deep Water Port	50.6	Signed (2007)
Sri Lanka	17	Hambantota Port	14.7	Biggest Trading Partner, Negotiations Started in 2014

Source: Mukherjee, 2018

A pertinent issues is the aspect of dual use of the ports controlled by China, to be used for military and surveillance activities, possibly threatening or positioning itself against the national security interest of India. Moreover, the issues of protecting the sea lanes of communication (SLOC), especially the chokepoints like the tiny waterway between Indonesia and Singapore, known as the Malacca Strait are pertinent for China. China intends to circumvent these issues by taking over control of ports and bases at very strategic locations, one which does have serious implications in the neighbourhood, especially India. The recent Belt and Road Initiative (BRI), whereby the 'road' passes through the ocean while the 'belt' passes through the land, is an important framework established by China in the 21st century. Here adhering to this, Chinese initiative to integrate various countries, have but expounded debt traps, leading to temporary but long-term implications to India. The semi-territoriality aspects of modern-day sovereignty in relation to BRI through the huge reserves of cash China hold is one that India cannot compete 'tit for tat'. But, the extension of assertiveness in South China Sea towards the Indian Ocean, or what the Sino-Russian scholars call as the Afro-Bengal Region are but a cause for concern for India. This is intended at gradually and incrementally displacing India's traditional hold over the vast ocean, one which has been argued as a colonialist fervor of the British in the pre-independence period. By using the Maritime Silk Road as an option and path to establish the modern-day 'tribute system', China intents to create dependencies all over the Indo-Pacific region. The increasingly inward-looking USA, fragmented European Union (EU) as well as segmented South Asian (and particularly South East Asian) nations do provide China with a greater leverage in gaining control over the maritime domain. The near century-old leasing of Sri Lankan port, dual-use possibilities of Gwadar port in Pakistan as part of the China-Pakistan Economic Corridor and the rise of Chinese control over foreign policy imperatives of other countries have hindered the traditional coherence of multiple points of security in the maritime domain. This increases the pressure of providing with regional security architecture in the maritime domain, one which 'the Quad', i.e. India, USA, Japan and Australia are in-adept to deal with as of now. The gap in coordination and information sharing, due to both security and/or economic reasons provide hindrances and vulnerabilities in the existing mechanisms. This has serious implications on the pattern of trade and commerce, most of which mainly occurs through the sea and oceans. Moreover, Chinese increasing assertiveness in the maritime domain that traditionally converges with Indian security apparatus and understanding of framework (Erickson, 2008; Mukherjee, 2018).

The conceptualization and operationalization of "strategic buffer zones" in the maritime domain has been integrated into the theory and practice of "Great Power Politics." The present scenario, wherein the maritime powers like the US, as well as China, have both inherently put in place, major strategic outposts to entail the military concept of "anti-access and area denial" (A2/AD) strategy. This is not just militarily viable but a greater deterrent against untimely aggressions or attacks from adversaries. A number of efforts are undertaken by India and its partner countries US, Japan and others in providing security, increasing coordination, information sharing and coherence within the maritime sector. The eastern region of the Pacific Ocean has always and still acts as a natural barrier, with strategic benefits against any aggressions or attacks against the US, one which still holds water in its military doctrines. But the South China Sea or East China Sea, historically doesn't and have not provided China with any form of natural barrier, as seen in the often escalated crisis through the Taiwan Strait. This is more pertinent in the current context where the US have developed the Freedom of Navigation Operations (FONOPS) under the Obama Administration and have been recurringly utilized by the Trump Administration as well (Mukherjee, 2018; Panda, 2019).

India: Strategic Options and Way Forward

India should increasingly look as well as develop the options to wend off aggressions and dominations by China. Indian policies should be strategically designed to deal with, in any case, of possible depredations to its national security. Moreover, the strategic spaces should be taken over, any void filled to provide strategic autonomy to Indian cause. With the increasing alignment of the US towards India, the traditional bonhomie between India and ASEAN countries, and the distaste towards China's hegemonic activities in the maritime domain, there is a cause and a need for Indian assertiveness as well. This assertiveness should be based on an increasing security preparedness by India in the maritime domain, particularly the Navy and to some lesser extent the Coast Guard. Moreover, the funding and technological imperatives should be increased to position Indian security apparatus at most strategic locations. India should recognize the various possibilities and strategic advantages of partnership with maritime powers like the US, Japan and European nations in providing an overall regional security architecture in the Indo-Pacific. Any form of inward-looking by India, or isolationist tendencies would only lead to further security deadlocks or checkmates from the Chinese counterparts, one which is largely the cause of concern in economic investments in Africa and Asia. Though the Cold War mentality of the US, should to a larger extent be avoided by India in dealing with China, this should in anyway hinder Indian aspirations in engagement with various small powers in the region, even if it means militarily as well. Historically, the Indira Gandhi Government and to a lesser extent Rajiv Gandhi have had India to engage in military-cum-security relationships with the small powers in the region, and India need not shy away from it as well. The strategic positioning of Indian maritime forces, and the ability to maneuver chokepoints or sloc in the Indian Ocean region should be leveraged to the greatest extent at required times to prevent belligerent tendencies from China. India's options to induce the operationalization of logistics and connectivity with both the European as well as other powers in the region could be used to its benefit in increasingly utilizing the maritime resources and domain to its benefit. Rather than going one-on-one with China in terms of military and economic spending, India could utilize the international and regional bonhomie by institutionalizing naval cooperation with various powers, while reducing the need for diverting resources for military purposes, while increasing investments for energy security, growth and development of the country.

References

Bhattacharjee, Shilavadra (2019). 23 Important Maritime Codes Used in the Shipping Industry. Retrieved from https://www.marineinsight.com/maritime-law/21-important-codes-used-in-the-shipping-industry/.

Bloomberg. (2017). China's 'blue water' navy catching up with the US. Retrieved fromhttps://www.straitstimes.com/asia/east-asia/chinas-blue-water-navy-catching-up-with-the-us.

Chuanying, Lu.(2016). China's Emerging Cyberspace Strategy, *The Diplomat*.Retrieved from https://thediplomat.com/2016/05/chinas-emerging-cyberspace-strategy/.

China Rescue and Salvage Association (CRSA).(2018). China International Rescue & Salvage Conference (CIRSC).Retrieved from http://www.cirsc.org.cn/en/index.aspx.

Deshpande, Vikrant. (ed.). (2018). *Hybrid Warfare: The Changing Character of Conflict*. New Delhi: Pentagon Press.

Gilbert, Gregory P. (2008). *Ancient Egyptian Sea Power and the Origin of Maritime Forces*. Commonwealth of Australia: Canberra.

Erickson, Andrew S. (2008). The Growth of China's Navy: Implications for Indian Ocean Security*.*Strategic Analysis*, 32(4), https://doi.org/10.1080/09700160802214425.

Fish, Isaac Stone.(2016). Crouching Tiger, Sleeping Giant. *Foreign Policy*. Retrieved from https://foreignpolicy.com/2016/01/19/china_shakes_the_world_cliche/.

Kane, Thomas M. (2002). *Chinese Grand Strategy and Maritime Power*. New York: Routledge.

Liangyu. (2018). China Focus: China's maritime economy expands by 7.5 pct in recent five years. Retrieved from http://www.xinhuanet.com/english/2018-01/21/c_136913316.htm.

Masuda, Masayuki. (2013). *China's Maritime Strategy and Maritime Law Enforcement Agencies: Quest for Maritime Power.*ANU-NIDS Joint Research Project.

Mukherjee, Tuneer. (2018). China's maritime quest in the Indian Ocean: New Delhi's options. Retrieved from https://www.orfonline.org/research/china-maritime-quest-in-the-indian-ocean-new-delhi-options/.

Panda, Ankit. (2019). US Navy Conducts First Freedom of Navigation Operation of 2019 in South China Sea. Retrieved from https://thediplomat.com/2019/01/us-navy-conducts-first-freedom-of-navigation-operation-of-2019-in-south-china-sea/.

Pharis, William D. J. (2009). China'sPursuitofaBlue-WaterNavy.United States Marine Corps.Retrieved from https://apps.dtic.mil/dtic/tr/fulltext/u2/a510462.pdf.

Sempa, Francis P. (2014). The Geopolitical Vision of Alfred Thayer Mahan. Retrieved from https://thediplomat.com/2014/12/the-geopolitical-vision-of-alfred-thayer-mahan/.

Sparks, John B. (1997).*Histomap of World History.*Chicago: Rand McNally & Co.

Sun, C., Li, X., Zou, W., Wang, S., & Wang, Z. (2018). Chinese Marine Economy Development: Dynamic Evolution and Spatial Difference. *Chinese Geographical Science*, 28(1), 111–126. doi:10.1007/s11769-017-0912-8.

To, Wai-Ming & Lee, Peter K. C. (2018).China's Maritime Economic Development: A Review, the Future Trend, and Sustainability Implications. *Sustainability* 10(12), 4844.https://doi.org/10.3390/su10124844.

UNESCAP.(1998). Maritime Safety Transport.Retrieved from https://www.unescap.org/sites/default/files/3.3%20China%20Presentation.pdf.

Xiao, Ming. (2000). China maritime safety administration in the newmillennium: challenges and strategies, *Dissertation*. Retrieved from https://commons.wmu.se/cgi/viewcontent.cgi?article=1423&context=all_dissertations.

Xinhua. (2000). China Improves Maritime Safety Administration. Retrieved from http://www.china.org.cn/english/5595.htm.

Air Power To Counter Maritime Terrorism

- Gp Capt A V Chandrasekaran (Retd.)

The undertaking of terrorist acts and activities, within the maritime environment, using or against vessels or fixed platforms at sea or in port, or against any one of their passengers or personnel, against coastal facilities or settlements, including tourist resorts, port areas and port towns or cities.

–Council for Security Cooperation in the Asia Pacific

Introduction:

Not long ago during the Second World War, airpower earned its spurs and glory over water. The theory of Maritime interdiction— attack of ships— was a major mission for decades in various decisive battles. From Brigadier General William Billy Mitchell's sinking of *Ostfriesland* on 21 July 1921[1] to the Battle of Midway in 1942, the use of airpower over water made for some dramatic turning points and altered the course of history. "Open and Stable Seas" constitute the basis for peace and prosperity of the international community as a whole. On date the threat of maritime terrorism looms large all around the globe and especially in the turbulent waters of Asia.

An act akin to the dramatic attack on 9/11 where in civilian commercial aircraft was used as a cruise missile to perpetuate one of the biggest acts of terror would pale in comparison to acts of maritime terror wherein large luxury cruisers with a huge tourist population can be targeted to inflict mass casualties, or huge oil tankers targeted to choke the vital sea lanes of communications (SLOCs) thereby causing a massive infringement in commercial marine traffic. Both these acts would ensure that the terrorists would get the publicity they hope for thereby motivating more cadres to join the terrorist outfits.

The 2008 attacks in Mumbai, India, was another reminder terrorists could exploit relatively open harbours to wreak havoc. To offset these threats the essence of an effective platform which can respond almost immediately, detect, interdict, and effect a decisive counter attack, with adequate pay load capabilities would be an ideal countermeasure. The element of airpower would be the answer to all maritime terrorism woes as it possesses all the above mentioned capabilities and more in abundance. In the words of former secretary of state Hilary Clinton "We may be dealing with a 17th century crime, but we need to bring 21st century solutions to bear." The air power has an array of unmanned aerial vehicles, both armed and unarmed, helicopters and amphibious planes to be extremely persistent and be precise in its targeting.

Clear perspectives on the nature and likelihood of specific types of maritime terrorist attacks are essential for prioritizing the nation's maritime anti-terrorism activities. In practice, however, there has been considerable public debate about the likelihood of scenarios frequently given high priority by federal policymakers, such as nuclear or "dirty" bombs smuggled in shipping containers, liquefied natural gas (LNG) tanker attacks, and attacks on passenger ferries. Differing priorities set by port officials, grant officials, and legislators lead to differing allocations of port security resources and levels of protection against specific types of attacks. How they ultimately relate to one another under a national maritime security strategy remains to be seen. Maritime terrorist threats to India are varied, and so are the nation's efforts to combat them.

Maritime Terror

The sea attracts terrorists like bees to a hive. Is it the numerous opportunities it serves to terrorists on a platter, the mystic aura it carries around or the element of secrecy it can offer to terrorists with little or no defences that has drawn the terrorists in is a point for serious debate. To perpetuate any act of terror one requires weapons both the gun variety and the explosive variety both which could be effectively smuggled using the vastness of the sea with ease from one point to another. This also facilitates clandestine movement of the chosen cadres from safe sanctuaries to the point of action. This transshipment could be from one country to another or even one continent to another. Terrorists fully realise that all acts of terror cost money from procurement to bribing of corrupt officials, paying blood money to the families of the so called martyrs and purchase of publicity. The smuggling of high value narcotics provide an ideal and easy alternate for a steady supply of funds flowing into the terror coffer. They also have a through realisation of how a crippling effect it can have on global economy when specific acts of economic terrorism can be carried out. This they do after carefully choosing targets after a continued surveillance and a careful study of intended consequences. The poor border controls and insufficient maritime domain awareness, facilitate terrorist groups to often operate unimpeded. Pakistan has a long history in providing its proxy militias with sophisticated weapon systems.

The most worrisome aspect is the smuggling of a dirty bomb or WMD material in a container to an intended theatre of operations that can lead to devastating consequences. No maritime attack on the high seas can be farfetched as the terrorists make up in numbers and motivation. The location and layout of ports often inhibit security measures, while berthed or anchored ships with unarmed crews are vulnerable targets, an aspect that is exploitable by organised crime and terrorists. Ships can also be high-profile targets offering considerable political and propaganda value. The attack on the USS Cole in Aden in 2000 has shown that even highly sophisticated warships can be threatened by low-tech attacks. Acts of maritime terrorism may have many objectives. They may seek to cause human casualties, economic losses, environmental damage, or other negative impacts, alone or in combination, of minor or major consequence. Terrorists can also develop effective attack capabilities relatively quickly using explosives-laden suicide boats and light aircraft; merchant and cruise ships as kinetic weapons to ram another vessel, warship, port facility, or offshore platform; commercial vessels as launch platforms for missile attacks; underwater swimmers to infiltrate ports; and unmanned underwater explosive delivery vehicles. Mines are also an effective weapon. Terrorists can also take advantage of a vessel's legitimate cargo, such as chemicals, petroleum, or liquefied natural gas, as the explosive component of an attack. Vessels can be used to transport powerful conventional explosives or WMD for detonation in a port or alongside an offshore facility.

Likely Targets of Maritime Terror

There are nine coastal states and four union territories in India which share maritime boundaries. It also houses around 3600 fishing villages and about 2.5 Crore people live within 50 km off the coast. This mind boggling figure is a testimony to the threat the seas can pose to any perpetuators of maritime terror. The targets can be multiple ranging from high value national assets, to a highly incendiary economic asset and can also cause serious human and ecological casualties.

Critical Coastal Targets

Some of the targets may encompass of the following;

i) Explosions of both conventional and unconventional in the vicinity of the ports.

ii) Off shore oil platforms in Mumbai and Gujarat Coasts.

iii) Oil Refineries situated all along like the ones of Jamnagar.

iv) Nuclear Power Stations like Kalpakkam, Kudankulam, Trombay etc.

v) Missile Testing Establishments in Chandipur fortunately being located in the less vulnerable eastern shores of the country.

vi) Warships and Nuclear powered submarines of the Indian Navy both stationary and while in sail.

vii) Passenger ferries or Luxury Cruisers (though many do not sail under an Indian flag) all with potential to inflict mass casualties.

viii) Choking vital maritime transit points through planned explosion and sinking of ship blocking the waterway leading to economic chaos.

The above are some of the targets which one could visualise but given the ingenuity of the terrorists the targets can be anything least intended. All these require careful guarding and counter methods to prevent any attack which are cost and labour intensive. In a growing economy like India the cost of these preventive measures can drain the exchequer thereby diverting valuable national resources.

Means of Maritime Terror

i) **Cargo Containers.** Cargo containers poses the single largest threat because it is difficult for anyone to know exactly what is inside a container as is called *Bomb in the Box scenario*. The cargo containers can be effectively used for smuggling chemical, biological or even radiological materials to carry out attacks at ports. The possibility of lone wolf attacker inside a container with adequate oxygen supply and a sizeable quantity of explosives or with radiological dispersion devices ("dirty" bombs) is also considered among the gravest maritime terrorism scenarios and can cause untold mayhem when a suicide act is attempted and successful. The worst part is India till date does not have Radiation Portal scanners fully operational to scan the containers well in sea before they are brought in. Container scanning has to be improved and enforced at all ports.

ii) **Trojan Horse Tactics.** History has some monumental examples. We can seldom forget the legendary and the beautiful Helen of Troy. It is an innovate tactic of high class subterfuge by the Greeks having a huge wooden horse filled with soldiers inside which was placed outside the gates of Troy. The Trojans thinking the Greeks had sailed away pulled the horse inside the city and the rest is history. What could not be achieved by a ten year siege was quickly accomplished by a classic act of subterfuge and deceit. On similar lines in the current context cache of weapons including explosives, communication equipment can be effectively concealed in innocent or innocuous looking vessels mainly fishing trawlers, tugs or resupply ships. All these variants of sailing vessels fall under a non-verifiable category of less than 500 tonnes. The International Ship and Port Facility Security (ISPS) excludes vessels less than 500 tonnes, and also accords a blanket clearance for all fishing vessels regardless of their size which can be well exploited by the terrorists.

iii) **Hijack of Vessel.** It was in March 2003, terrorists had hijacked a chemical tanker off the coast of Sumatra using time tested pirate techniques and then manoeuvred the vessel in a learning pattern to control the sailing of the ship. This set alarm bells going and a detailed study opined that the 'pirates' or 'terrorists' had taken control of the MV Dewi Madrim and during that time had altered course and speed and tried various mid-sea manoeuvres to check whether they would be in complete control of the ship.[2] The conclusion drawn was that they had been learning to control a ship in the same way that the 11 September hijackers had learnt to fly aircraft almost eight years later, possibly with a similar purpose in mind. An attempt to hijack the Pakistani Naval Warship PNS Zulfiqar in September 2014, by Lt Jakhrani a 26 year old dismissed naval officer and three accomplices in Karachi was thwarted, but could have had disastrous consequences as the terrorists had inside support which facilitated their easy entry into the closely guarded harbour. Their aim was to seize the Frigate and during the Naval exercise with the US Navy target the USS Supply a refuelling tanker using on-board the eight C-802 anti-ship missiles on the frigate to cause mayhem. A number of serving officers and sailors were arrested and eight were sentenced to death for treason. Similarly PNS Aslat was to be hijacked for use against Indian warships.[3] The fearsome threat from the hijacked vessels still looms large and enhanced security of both military and merchant ships is a must to do.

iv) **Destruction of ships at choke-points**-The Biblical story of David and Goliath amply illustrates that even the most intimidating and formidable enemy can be defeated by a weaker but smarter opponent. David's adept use of a simple weapon like a sling shot at the right time and place earned him a stunning and unexpected victory. The enduring lesson of this Biblical story should not be lost to powerful military forces of today. A case in study is the successful attack on USS Cole in the harbour of Aden causing huge human causalities and effectively crippling the warship. It goes to prove that a relatively weak but determined and intelligent adversary, skilfully employing force at the right time and the right place, may prevail against a much stronger foe. Therefore, it is but essential that prudent military planners must anticipate those situations that place a powerful force at risk. Terrorists need to be lucky just once unlike the counter terrorism operators who have to be lucky all time to prevent an attack. Chokepoint passage represents an operational situation where the significant power of a blue-water navy is extremely vulnerable—even against a relatively weak coastal force. The hijacking and blowing up a vessel in a choke point can have devastating consequences. Currently, globally there are about 200 straits and channels which connects bigger water bodies. However, fortunately, and strategically only eight of them can be categorised as 'choke points', which either shorten largely sailing routes or are the only gate enabling to go out to other maritime areas. These include: the Suez Canal, the Panama Canal, the Strait of Gibraltar, the Turkish straits (The Bosporus and the Dardanelles), the Danish straits (Great Belt, Little Belt, and Oresund), the Strait of Hormuz, the Bab El-Mandab, and the Strait of Malacca. It is needless to emphasise the huge importance of mentioned straits and channels to maritime economy. The Strait of Malacca is the second largest choke point in the world in terms of the quantity of transported oil. The Strait of Malacca with Singapore constitutes one of the most critical choke points on the planet. [4] Closing or at least a temporary blockade of Malacca can result in traversing hundreds of kilometers extra out of compulsion and operational necessity or can lead to a total transport paralysis. Even a temporary blockade of shipping Choke Points may shake the economic security globally and, more precisely, may cause a significant increase in total costs of the energy.

v) **Hijacking a LNG carrier as a floating bomb- This is a distant possibility but cannot be shrugged away.** Larger tankers, LNG carriers and chemical tankers and ships with volatile cargoes (e.g. ammonium nitrate) can all be used to cause mayhem when blown closer to shore. However for ensuring success a smaller tanker, LPG carrier, or chemical carrier might be a better prospect, although the extent of damage caused might be less than that from an attack on a larger vessel. Smaller vessels can be more easily hijacked, after overpowering their smaller crews, it might even be possible to hide the fact from port authorities that the vessel had been hijacked and crewed by terrorists. A chemical or LNG tanker attacked by missiles or rockets near a port facility or populated urban area, and if its cargo released into the atmosphere, could have deadly consequences. LNG tankers have the fearsome potential, if attacked, to create superheated fireballs and can create sizeable human and economic damage and their sheer size and audacity, can truly terrorize both the target population and the international community as a whole.

vi) **Suicide attack by speed boats-**The suicide small boat attacks on the tanker Limburg and the USS Cole, as well as attempted attacks on other US warships, amplify that speedboats may be "emerging as the weapon of choice" of maritime terrorists. While these small craft offer advantages in terms of speed, stealth and surprise, there also has to be some qualifications as to where such attacks are likely. The LTTE had perfected the art of suicide ramming by its Black Tigers to cause a huge damage to the Sri Lankan Navy. The Houthis have also tried to use these tactics for economic warfare, targeting an Aramco oil distribution terminal in the Red Sea on the Saudi coast, just north of Yemen, using a high-speed boat laden with explosives.

vii) **Mass Casualty in Cruise Ship-**The possibilities of attacks on cruise ships, is a nightmare considering the causalities and the subsequent mayhem it may cause. The broader range of likely attacks on a cruise ship, may include an on-board bombing, followed by standoff artillery assaults and food or water contamination scenarios, and these present the greatest combination of threat and vulnerability. On analysis, all of the attack modes targeting cruise ships involve roughly comparable estimates of potential economic harm which would be the main intent, but parasitic bombings, ramming attacks with IEDs, and biological attacks (i.e., those involving contamination of a ship's food or water supply) are projected as presenting somewhat greater potential for harm in the form of human casualties spreading fear among populace.

viii) **Airborne & Aquatic Drones-** The application and usage of drones for tactical purposes was the preserve of security agencies. As technology became increasingly commercialised for myriad purposes, malicious non-state actors such as terrorists and criminals have begun circumventing international trade regulations that restrict the transfer of potentially dual-use technologies including drones. The ISIS building drones from scratch in Iraq and its lethal use and in Southeast Asia, the Maute Group also known as the Islamic State of Lanao, a radical Islamist group composed of former Moro Islamic Liberation Front guerrillas and foreign fighters led by Omar Maute, the alleged founder of a Dawlah Islamiya, reportedly deployed commercial off-the-shelf drones to gain a tactical advantage in urban warfare in Marawi city, Philippines against the Philippine security forces. The Houthis in Yemen have used remote-controlled boat bombs, the first time on 30 January 2017, against a Saudi Navy frigate, killing two Saudi sailors.

Terrorists have reportedly retrofitted aerial drones to conduct attacks and surveillance and aquatic drones could be retrofitted to function as remotely controlled or autonomous waterborne improvised explosive devices. The proliferation of aquatic drones may plausibly widen the terrorists' capabilities and opportunities for attacks to coastal cities. Aquatic drones are unmanned marine vehicles which may be autonomous or remotely operated and these drones operate either on or under the water surface. While the misuse of aerial drones (UAVs) for urban terrorism is a current security concern, it would also be of strategic importance to monitor the developments of aquatic drones for surface and underwater operations. The aquatic drones could easily shift the maritime terrorism landscape by drastically reducing terrain challenges and enhancing terrorists' capability to launch seaborne attacks.

Such attacks could be aimed at strategic and soft targets such as civilian passenger vessels, port facilities, tourist and sea sports hubs, and large-scale public events by the sea.[5] The aquatic drones has the ability to manoeuvre unseen until they are in a position to attack according them a huge tactical advantage in ensuring a greater degree of success. It is also ironical that most of the security agencies world over involved in anti-terror operations have force protection measures against surface and not sub-surface threats especially from the drones. If the undersea network cables are attacked they can cause massive global disruption.

Protection Priorities

The public are at liberty and may raise questions concerning the relationship among the nation's various maritime security activities, and the implications of differing protection priorities among them. Improved gathering and sharing of maritime terrorism intelligence may enhance consistency of policy and increase efficient deployment of maritime security resources. In addition, the Government of India may assess how the various elements of Indian maritime security fit together in the nation's overall strategy to protect the public from terrorist attacks

Airpower as a countermeasure

With a shift away from the emphasis on conventional responsibilities, navies are redefining their roles. The complexity of maritime threats, specifically from non-state actors, and the current nature of maritime violence have demanded a new set of naval responses, causing the traditional distinction between the conventional and constabulary roles of navies to wither. The Indian Navy and the ICG fully realise the gravity of the situation and are increasingly turning towards the medium of air to counter these type of threats by non-state actors.

Airpower when deployed on a full spectrum offers a flexible, timely and a lethal strike capability, including a new generation of highly discriminate weapons. It also affords the least politically risky of the military options for striking back at terror, especially maritime terror because it does not entail putting troops on the water or moving significant naval asset[s] in harm's way. Moreover, the high speed of response associated with airpower will become increasingly important as terrorists acquire the capabilities to move swiftly from one theatre to another and to attack with little or no warning.

Air power can accomplish this through scaring by regular low level buzzing, or starving—demoralizing the enemy, through displays of might or destruction, to the point where fighting seems useless, or destroying the enemy's supplies to the point where further fighting is effectively impossible. "Frightening your enemy is the fundamental and presumably the oldest weapon of war," Peter Calvocoressi, Guy Wint, and John Pritchard wrote in *Total* War.[6]

The employment of airpower in counter-terror frameworks is based on the theory of "find, fix and finish", and aviation researchers Adam R. Grissom and Karl P. Mueller correctly point out, a force's aerial intelligence, surveillance and reconnaissance (ISR) capabilities are in fact the first line of offence against terror from the sea.

Aerial Platforms

In order to achieve the desired level of success air power has five variants each one which has a unique characteristic to take on maritime terror. The variants vary from the manned to the unmanned from the heavy to the featherweight and the high-speed to the slow flying and from the fixed wing to the rotary variants.

Unmanned Aerial Vehicles

Unmanned Aerial Vehicles (UAVs) have been referred to variously as drones, robot planes, pilotless aircraft, Remotely Piloted Vehicles (RPVs), Remotely Piloted Aircrafts (RPAs), and other terms, which describe aircrafts that fly under the control of an operator with no person on board. The drones unlike the rockets and missiles can execute controlled landings and undertake repeated flights. They are most often called UAVs, and when combined with ground control stations and data links, form unmanned aerial systems (UAS) or lethal autonomous weapons systems (LAWS).[7] The drones are generally equipped with electro-optic, infrared and high-resolution video cameras that can track both stationary and moving targets in the sea. There are a variety of drones ranging from the micro and mini UAVs, to the tactical UAVs, the strategic UAVs, and the special task UAVs. This fundamentally rewrote the rules of battle—power projection with minimal vulnerability became possible.

The drones to counter the terrorists can be both shore and ship launched. It is also effective, handy and incurs a low cost because it needs no extra facilities on the ship to get airborne and land back. Most of the attack by the terrorists often occurs in the night to gain the element of surprise with a small boat, so the drone should have a thermo camera to detect human beings or an outboard engine in the dark. It brings a rare ability to catapult from the deck of a surface ship and perform vital forward-operating reconnaissance missions, and it adds a significant sphere of new variables to India's marine forces strategic and tactical approach.

First and foremost, deploying drones from naval ships enables a wider and longer surveillance reach to identify terrorists, small boat threats, piracy and drug trafficking. Woven into this is a fast-growing ability to network real-time video data with both Indian Navy assets and Coast Guard "nodes" such as helicopters. Such a technical advance allows the service to operate in a wider, more dispersed, yet networked fashion. The surveillance drone, for instance, can locate sea mines dropped by the terrorists as was observed in the Persian Gulf recently, enemy movements and even small boat sailing in a belligerent fashion, and could much more quickly cue the Navy, therefore greatly expediting the needed military response. It brings automatic surface search and cueing sensors, enabled by intelligence and air support. Following this conceptual trajectory, particularly when it comes to securing the India's vast vulnerable coast and EEZ, and global maritime hotspots, it does not seem beyond the realm to envision a scenario wherein a surveillance drone comes across an enemy attack submarine attempting surveillance near or in Indian territorial waters. With drones performing extended ISR, the Coast Guard could cue Navy anti-submarine vessels, helicopters and other air assets to rapidly deploy. The usage of submarines to transport trained aqua terrorists by Pakistan cannot be ruled out.[8] The drone can give real time intelligence to an attacking Marine Commando team of the Indian Navy about the strength and weapon holding of the intended target as they have the ability to operate in the close vicinity of the target. Indian Navy does not have an armed drone in its inventory and in future if acquired can identify and take a target out as well. They can be used for Intelligence preparation for an operational environment (IPOE), and can also designate targets using laser markers for attacks by laser bombs or precision missiles by both fixed wing and rotary wing aircraft of the Indian defence forces. It has an additional advantage of negating the human factor thereby minimising risk to the aircrew, and data transmitted can be analysed live for any corrective or coercive action.

Role of Armed Unmanned Aerial Vehicles

1   The armed UAV can be deployed in a standalone mode.

2   The UAVs ability to loiter and gather intelligence, before a strike is a key to its employment.

3   The basic concept underlying in deployment of armed UAVs is to quickly kill an emerging target before it disappears back into hiding.

4   Kill Chain is the process that prescribes the sequence of events needed to locate, identify and destroy the target. All these actions can be completed by an armed UAV.

5   The tactical advantage in arming the UAV was that the sensor and shooter were resident in the same platform and no dissemination of information was required resulting in a speedier response from the moment of sighting a target to the delivery of the weapon.

Role of the Rotary

The helicopter's technical-tactical characteristics, the ability to fly at very low heights (which makes it hard to be detected by the opponent) and the execution of the stationary flight above the target, as well as the unique capability to land in any place, regardless of the state and characteristics of the land or ships, was immediately exploited by the armed forces. Thus, the helicopter became the ideal platform for mobility and for supporting ground forces in general and Special Forces operations (SOF) in particular. In addition due its flexible characteristics helicopters can be integrally utilized in the air, on land and at sea seamlessly to conduct a plethora of anti-terror operations.[9]

Helicopters can operate from unprepared airfields, an advantage over fixed-wing aircraft which require a longer, prepared runway. It can also hover at low altitudes for longer periods of time – a suitable platform for conducting UUVs (under water unmanned vehicles) surveillance operations from the air.

Its operational parameters allow it tooperate from frigates, destroyers, cruisers, amphibious ships and aircraft carriers, and is suitable for intense littoral warfare operations for handling numerous contacts in confined spaces, and for open-water operations. For attack operations at sea, helicopters are used in close cooperation with the ships, both independently and in coordination with other ships or aircraft. Its capabilities also include ASAC (Airborne Surveillance and Control Area), SAR (search and rescue) and troop transport to areas of conflict. Once a ship carrying inimical elements are identified Anti surface ships (ASuW) operations, to deter, and neutralize can be immediately initiated. It can also initiate maritime surveillance (MSO), operations procedures at sea (MWO), naval gunfire support (NGFS), communications relay, logistics support and personnel transfer and vertical replenishment (VERTREP) all of which have a lasting impact on maritime anti-terror roles.

The possibility of a situation involving terrorists prepared to die on a suicide mission during execution of their plans, demands a speedy elimination of the threat. The helicopters conduct advanced force generation activities both ashore and at sea, in order to prepare maritime helicopter aircrew and maintenance personnel to deploy at a moment's notice in support of anti-terror operations. The deployment of an adaptable and versatile platform such as the helicopter has all the potential of having a profound and terrifying effect on the developing terror situation. The versatile helicopter despite its vulnerability to small arms fire is one of the best platforms to attain favourable asymmetry is such situations, in order to limit the damage and preserve precious trained human resource in addition to the other critical assets.[10]

The advanced navigation and ship landing aids enable the helicopter to perform safe landings in day/night even under adverse weather conditions. The operations are further supplemented by a deck lock device for securing the touchdown in high sea states. India has Kamov 28, and the Sea King and the ICG has the ALH MK III. The Ka-28 operated by the Indian Navy are equipped with rappelling kit (for simultaneous landing of four troops) and a pintle mount in the port door for a side-firing 7.62mm machine gun. These machines are useful for long-range armed patrols and boarding operations, and they also retain full sea SAR capabilities. The recently acquired Apache Gunships has an oversea capacity and is fit for maritime operations, potentially enabling naval strikes on terrorists.

Role of fixed wing aircraft in anti-terror operations

Fixed wing aircrafts have two variants the fighter and the transport version. In addition, they also perform various operational duties including maritime surveillance, airborne early warning, aerial refuelling, and even operates against targets under water. The fighter variant of the aircrafts including the maritime Sukhoi 30, and Jaguars of the Indian Air Force, and the MIG-29s of the Indian Navy are all lethal platforms and when introduced in the battle scene can have a devastating effect on the terrorists. Today, Indian Air Force use modern, lightweight inertial measuring units, positioning data from satellites such as the Global Positioning System (GPS) constellation, and sometimes, terminal homing sensors to guide weapons to their targets, it becomes easy for the fighter aircrafts when warned about an impending maritime terror attack from an inbound vessel to take it out without putting own forces in danger. The high speed of these aircrafts along with the accuracy can have a deadly effect on the adversaries.[11]

The fixed wing fleet of the Indian Navy is equipped with the IL-38, & P-8I Neptune variant of the aircrafts. It is noteworthy that India is the only country to use the P8I other than the United States of America. The Indian Coast Guard has the modified Dornier which is ideally suited for maritime patrol roles. These aircrafts form a punch to the air power over water with multi mission maritime patrol capabilities, and is the Indian Navy's sea shield concept. The P8-I Armed with deadly harpoon block-II missiles, MK-54 lightweight torpedoes, rockets and depth charges, free-fall bombs, sensor and radar-packed aircraft are the country's "intelligent hawk eyes".[12]

The aircraft is fully integrated with state-of-the-art sensors and highly potent anti-surface and anti-submarine with a maximum speed of 907 kmph and an operating range of over 1,200 nautical miles, "with four hours on station", the P-8I will be able to detect "threats" — and neutralize them if required — far before they come anywhere near Indian shores. The aircraft is further endowed with the capability for round the clock, all-weather surveillance through sensor suites and can be ideally sho-re-based, airborne, or deployed on buoys and offshore platforms, as well on shore-based elevated platforms capable of carrying out open ocean surveillance as well as coastal surveillance. It will also be able to integrate information provided by other sources like merchant navy and fishing trawlers, and has arear-view mirror with large observation windows & fuselage pylons to carry night search lights.

The Indian Navy is also in the process of acquiring Shinmaywa Us2I amphibious aircraft from Japan which also has multi role capabilities. It has a capacity to carry up to 20 passengers which can be Special Forces Operatives of MARCOS (Marine Commandos of the Indian Navy) land in the vicinity of identified threat with Gemini Inflatable boats for mounting an attack on the terrorists in the mid-sea. To protect itself from any enemy lethal action The Shinmaywa is equipped with formidable arsenal 6 Zuni rockets, torpedoes and even depth charges to neutralise under water drones. This version can be effectively deployed in the Andaman & Nicobar group of islands due to its inherent capability of rapid surveillance and prompt response. It can also reach out to locations faster than the ships and possesses the long range capability to detect, board, engage and eliminate the threats. It has the added advantage of operating from mainland to distant waters without even the need of a runway.

Grey areas over blue water

There are tremendous advantages of using airpower in countering maritime terror. However there are certain risks and impediments and they are outlined-;

1. There can be inherent delays owing to dissemination of information from the sensor (on the UAV) to the shooter (on the aircraft) being on different platforms can result in critical time delays.

2. The recovery of UAV's while rolling with the waves is risky. There would be a necessity of using advanced algorithms to account for the vessel's seaborne motion patterns

3. It has to be specifically ensured that the man machine mix is right simply implying that the right kind of man & right state of mind to man systems as he has to take critical decisions for destruction of enemy hostiles using missiles.

4. The UAVs & helicopters are prone to SAM (Surface to Air Missile) attacks, when attacked by multiple shooters.

5. Both the UAVs and the helicopters have fixed airborne time as they have to be refuelled for continuing operations.

6. The operations in adverse weather conditions, is restricted due to *line squall* an adverse meteorological phenomena which is highly detrimental in ocean flying.

7. These air platforms have limited payloads when confronting multiple boats.

Conclusion

With the threat of maritime terror increasing by the day is essential for India to shift gears and put its offensive capabilities in action. The abrogation of Article 370 in the state of Jammu and Kashmir is a warning for things to come from Pakistan. Pakistan a 100 year headache for India would be stepping up its kinetic operations against India. With most of the land based assets reasonably well guarded, the vulnerability lies in our vast coastline. With trained hydra terrorists Pakistan can exploit the sea lanes to mount operations against India. It is in this context all necessary acquisitions including armed UAVs, and the amphibious aircraft may be procured at the earliest to thwart these looming threats. There is also a necessity to further perfect the targeting capabilities using advanced technology to ensure there is no wastage of precious inventory. The night offensive capability also needs to be improved to identify and neutralize any stealthy approaches made in the wee hours. The government should shrug its inhibitions review its offensive doctrine and use the air power as an offensive platform as was witnessed in the recent Balakot attack.

Notes

1   General William "Billy" Mitchell and the Sinking of the Ostfriesland: A Consideration, Dominick Pisano https://airandspace.si.edu/stories/editorial/general-william-%E2%80%9Cbilly%E2%80%9D-mitchell-and-sinking-ostfriesland-consideration accessed on19 May 2019.

2   Peril on the sea, https://www.economist.com/business/2003/10/02/peril-on-the-sea, accessed on 19 May 19.

3   Five IS linked naval officers get death sentence in dockyard attack case, Malik Asad, https://www.dawn.com/news/1260340. Accessed on 12 May 2019.

4   Nincic D. J., Sea Lane Security and U.S. Maritime Trade: Chokepoints as Scarce Resources , Tangredi S. J. (dir.) Globalization and Maritime Power, National Defence University, Institute for National Strategic Studies, Washington (DC) 2002

5   Aquatic drone terror attacks a growing possibility *BY* **VS SUGUNA,** HTTPS://WWW.TODAYONLINE.COM/COMMENTARY/AQUATIC-DRONE-TERROR-ATTACKS-GROWING-POSSIBILITY, accessed on 12 May 19.

6   The Air Power Revolution, Michael Kelly, https://www.theatlantic.com/magazine/archive/2002/04/the-air-power-revolution/302462/ accessed on 12 May 2019.

7   Gertler, J. (2012). "Homeland Security: Unmanned Aerial Vehicles and Border Surveillance. Congressional Research Service". http://www.dtic.mil/cgi-bin/GetTRDoc?AD=ADA524297; Matthias Bieri and Marcel Dickow (2014), "Lethal Autonomous Weapons Systems: Future Challenges", CSS Analyses in Security Policy, No.164, November, accessed on 12 May 2019.

8   Drones for offshore and Maritime Missions: Opportunities and Barriers, Marrianne Harbo Fredrieksen, https://eicluster.dk/sites/default/files/publications/drones_for_offshore_and_maritime_missions_sdu_spring_2018.pdf, accessed on 12 May 2019.

9   Maritime Rotary Wing, The importance of helicopters for both naval and joint operations, Commander Paulo Florentino, Joint Air Power Competence Centre, https://www.japcc.org/maritime-rotary-wing/, accessed on 14 April 2019.

10   India, US to implement HOSTAC to strengthen maritime security, Times of India, 27 October 2017, https://timesofindia.indiatimes.com/india/india-us-to-implement-hostac-to-strengthen-maritime-security/articleshow/61254477.cms, accessed on 10 May 2019.

11   Flight Global, 14 August 2017, https://www.flightglobal.com/news/articles/upgraded-maritime-jaguar-makes-first-flight-440247/, accessed on 10 May 2019.

12   P8I "Neptune" India's Eye in the Sky, ArjunRaf, 8 October 2018, https://defencelover.in/p-8i-neptune-indian-navys-eye-in-the-sky/, accessed on 12 May 2019.

India's Maritime Policy in the context of Changing Asian Security Architecture

Aaradhana Singh

India has emerged as an important Asian power with the advent of 21st century. At the global level also, it has become an important player and sharing all important global and Asian multilateral platforms. Since the end of cold war, the locus of global system has started to tilt towards Asia and according to global economic pundits, Asia will be representing more than half of the global GDP. It has further changed the dynamics of bilateral and multilateral relations in Asia.

We are aware of the fact that a wide array of opinions was expressed since the end of the cold war on the idea that Asia will be an important player in the coming decades. At the end of the cold war, debates started on new lines by the formulators of foreign policy that both World system and Asian system must be multi-polar. This is one of the most significant issue where India and China diverge as China's underlying problem lies. China does not have a problem with world being multi-polar but it wants Asian balance of power to be unipolar super headed by China. Japan also thinks similar to Indian line and thus bilateral relationship between India and Japan has been deepening since the end of the cold war. India-Japan relationship has grown rapidly since last one decade. Due to inherent geo-political, economic and strategic dimensions this bilateral relationship is all set to reformulate new Asian balance of power based on multiplicity.

China, Japan, India and Vietnam are indulged in reformulating the balance of power within Asia. Other Asian countries also do not China's supremacy and thus their bonhomie with the competitors of China is deepening in an excellent manner since last one decade and all set to grow in the foreseeable future. In recent years, China has exposed its intention to use force to capture Islands under Japanese rule since many decades.

In various regions of China, protests had been organized against Japan including Hong Kong protests, which demanded capture of Japan ruled Islands in East China Sea. Including United States, India had also insisted amicable resolution of disputes and adherence to international law by all concerned parties. Due to border disputes with China, India has also been apprehensive about Chinese steps and that also has strengthened its bilateral relationship with Japan in a massive manner. These events vindicate that balance of power theory is working well in Asian theater and all set to sustain the process due to Chinese reluctance to accommodate the aspirations of other countries.

The new balance of power in Asia is all set to reshape existing power architecture. However, the theory of balance of power according to its proponents has come into being with the theory of Prisoner's Dilemma. Balance of power has been one of the most debated concepts of the international relations. The balance of power is a form of compromise among states that find its order preferable to absolute chaos, even though it is a system that favors the stronger and more prosperous states at the expenses of the weaker. Great powers play the dominant role in balance of power system because of their preponderant military force and their control of key technologies.[1] The cold war era just after the end of the Second World War is a classic example of balance of power between the United States and the Soviet Union. In the post-cold war era even the prevalence of the anarchic international environment has created a fear psychosis. Military build-ups and its competition by rival powers have left every harbinger of the international system insecure therefore all countries are trapped in a dilemma. This phenomenon is called the Security Dilemma.[2]

Right from Keshore Madhubani to several other pundits of international relations, everyone is discussing the emergence of an all-powerful Asia but the weighty question is why Asian powers are not cooperating and thus negating utopian idea of cooperation among Asian countries if we compare them with the European countries. China, India, Japan, South Korea, Indonesia, Iran and Vietnam are some of the important Asian powers. The changing power configuration in Asia has altered Nehru's hypothesis and Asia seems to follow European model of conflict, however the post second world war Europe has emerged as a beacon of cooperation and must be emulated by other regional groupings. Major Asian countries are not cooperating because of underlying divergence in interests among them. China wants its unipolar dominance over Asia but at the global level wants multi-polarity. India, Japan, South Korea, Indonesia, Iran and

Vietnam wanted both Asia and the globe to be multi-polar. Kautilaya, one of the earliest strategic thinkers had stated that convergences of interests are the base which determine a state's foreign policy. There are some common interests between India and Japan. This bilateral relationship could be one of the most deepening relationships of 21st century Asia. It is also relevant to be noted that they had an average relationship during the cold war. Even after cold war, 1998 Pokhran-II nuclear testings by India took the world by surprise. Many countries including Japan reacted sharply. It suspended all political exchanges and even economic assistance was frozen for nearly three years.

According to two leading foreign policy experts from China Institute of International Studies "India's border dispute with China have yet to be resolved and therefore it views a stronger relationship with Japan as a way to counter balance China's growing influence in the Asia-Pacific region."[3] As China's dispute with Japan escalates over Islands in East China Sea, China seems worried that India will throw its weight in favor of Tokyo. Chinese experts believe that India and Japan share much strategic common ground on China. First time probably in recent history, Chinese experts have accepted that India is working on the reciprocation of Chinese policy of encircling India within South Asia and therefore deepening its relationships with all estrange neighbour of China.[4]

India-United States relations have also deepened phenomenally since last two decades. Both were estranged allies during cold war era but today they have converted their relationship into that of being engaged allies. In June 2019, G-20 summit has taken place in Japan and besides normal business; sub group summit has taken place in the sidelines of G-20 summit. It is known as JAI (Japan, America and India). Growing India-United States relations have further propelled India-Japan and India-ASEAN relations as well. These strengthening alignments have further complicated the security architecture of Asia.

India is well settled in the midst of the Indian Ocean. It is the natural custodian of Indian Ocean. Indian Ocean has become extremely significant because more than half of the global trade commutes through it. It also connects South China Sea near Malacca Strait which is extended to Andaman Sea. South China Sea connects Indian Ocean to the Pacific Ocean. The growing economic activities have kept the entire sea route of communication extremely congested and it has given birth to new unwanted activities like piracy and others in the region.

Just after the end of the cold war, India's trade was hardly 30 billion dollar, which has reached above 800 billion dollar by the end of 2018. That also makes maritime policy of India quite important not only for India's comprehensive security but also for justice-based sea lanes of communication in the Indian Ocean and adjoining seas. This paper is, therefore, intending to dwell upon maritime issues in the context of changing security architecture of Asia and how India can cope up with the emerging challenges is moot research point of this paper.

The arrival of Modi government in 2014 has been a new hallmark in Indian politics because after 30 years, people of India gave single party majority to Modi led NDA. In November 2014, PM Modi declared the up gradation of Look East Policy into Act East Policy in India-ASEAN summit held in Myanmar. According to Daniel Rajendran, many saw it as a defining moment of India's Asia policy.[5]

Look East Policy was mooted by PM P. V. Narasimha Rao to consolidate Indian imprint in Southeast and East Asia given the enormous goodwill and soft power India possess in the region. Act East Policy is just an accelerated version of that process. First of all, it has upgraded the ambit from Myanmar to Australia; secondly, it insisted proactive mode instead of reactive and thirdly it has strategic components besides economic aspects.

At this juncture, security architecture in Asia has remained unstable. China is willing to dominate the narrative of sole supreme authority in Asia. India along with like-minded countries are opposing that idea. Interestingly United States, which had not been very cooperative with India during cold war era, has also been standing with India to keep Asia multipolar. It vindicates Kautilyan notion which proclaims that synergy of ideology cannot be cementing factor of international relations only synergy of national interests.

India has developed better than average trade relations with the countries of ASEAN and East Asia. ASEAN and East Asian countries have developed excellent trade relations with China but they have simultaneously been confronting with China because of trust deficit. South China Sea and East China Sea have emerged as flashpoint between China and the countries of its neighborhood. The countries of ASEAN and East Asia want India to act as a counterbalance to China in this region as China has both actively and passively challenged international norms and sovereignty claims in its neighbourhood. Traditionally, India has been considered a weak strategic power due to its slow decision-making process. Arrival of Modi in 2014 for the first term and its historic repeat in 2019 has infused a new momentum in the contours of India's foreign policy. Dokhlam (2017) and Balakot (2019) has emboldened Indian strategic imprints particularly in Asia. Modi government has adopted proactive foreign policy which is based on the ideals of realism instead of idealism. Post Dokhlam, PM Modi had met with Chinese President Xi Jinping in Wuhan for an informal summit. Both leaders met 11 times in last five years and President Xi Jinping is coming to India for another summit level talk with PM Modi in later part of 2019. At the same time India remains only country perhaps to oppose Chinese OBOR and other connectivity inter-continental projects.

Maritime policy remains at the core of India's newly calibrated proactive foreign policy being a natural guardian of the Indian Ocean. More than half of the international trade commutes through it. It also connects all important global sea lanes of communication. In recent years, India has upgraded its defense budget and substantial allocation have been made for the naval forces also. Although it is not enough given the fact that major fleets are ageing and need urgent replacements but even with less than required budget, Indian navy is known for its quality and competence and has shown its swiftness to ASEAN countries in the backdrop of 2004 Tsunami.

Since last few years, Indian navy has been extremely active in ASEAN, East Asia and larger plank of the Indo-Pacific. It has been one of the hallmarks of Act East Policy. Port calls, joint naval exercises and maritime capacity building programmes with friendly navies has uplifted India's geopolitical status in ASEAN and East Asia. Regular warships deploy in Bay of Bengal and the South China Sea has underlined India's nautical dimensions of India's Act East Policy. Regular and intense joint bilateral and multilateral naval exercises have underlined India's maritime interests in the Asia Pacific region.[6]

Indian trade has also gone up rapidly since the end of the cold war. Before cold war, India's overall trade was almost negligible but now it is roughly touching 1 trillion dollar. India needs justice based free sea lanes of communication for this purpose and needless to say that it is in larger interests of all important countries who have stakes in global trade. India has also shown enough courage to stand with the disputant countries of ASEAN on South China Sea and also stood with Japan on East China Sea issues. In both disputes China has negated the legitimate rights of the disputants and declared that South China Sea as its own territory and also refused to obey international tribunal order in 2016 in favour of Philippines. United States and many like-minded countries also stood with India on both disputes. It is not for curving out any territory in the region but for the compliance of relevant international laws. South China Sea has emerged as new bone of contention between China and disputant countries of ASEAN. "Never let a good crisis go to waste," the late British Prime Minister Winston Churchill advised. The Reed Bank crisis, which saw a suspected Chinese militia vessel sink a Philippine fishing boat in June 2019, has energised those who advocate upgrading the Philippine-US alliance.

Latest surveys show a growing number of Filipinos now favouring a tougher stance in the South China Sea and advocating for more cooperation with traditional allies against China.[7] Present Philippines President is a Chinese ally but due to changing public opinion he is under immense pressure to change his South China Sea policies. It will gravitate Philippines towards the United States which is proactive to ensure relevant international laws in South China Sea.

New Delhi has moved forward to strengthen strategic maritime relations with the littoral countries of ASEAN and East Asia and sought exclusive greater stability in power balance in maritime Asia. Indian navy has upgraded its ship deployment. In 2013, 4 ships were present in 4 countries but by 2017 the number has gone up to the presence of 17 ships in 17 countries.[8] Vietnam has emerged as the fulcrum of India's maritime policy in the ASEAN and India has invested much in the region and particularly enriched Vietnamese navy and has equipped Vietnamese navy with missiles. In return, Hanoi has permitted Indian warships to utilize its port services and also granted Indian oil company ONGC Videsh Limited to sustain extension to explore Vietnamese oil blocks in the disputed South China Sea waters within its territory which has been objected by the Chinese.[9] Likewise India has developed excellent relations with other maritime powers of ASEAN. Singapore has remained closest Indian maritime partner in the region and bilateral naval exercise with Singapore navy has been extremely successful particularly in the disputed South China Sea. India has also participated in bilateral naval exercises with Indonesia and Japan. In January 2016, Indian coast guard along with Japanese counterpart had a marathon joint naval exercise in the Bay of Bengal and observed a high level of functional synergy and coordination.[10] With Australia also, New Delhi has been involved sustainably particularly in trilateral naval exercises along with the United States and Japan. India had been hesitant to include Australia in the process initially but that hesitation has started to disappear. Indian leaders have recognised Canberra's acceptance of Indian's strategic ascendance and also their vastly converging interests in dealing with China's growing assertiveness in maritime Asia has been an important factor behind the deepening of their relationship.[11]

The moot challenge has been China's expanding maritime footprints. China has developed ports in Myanmar, Sri Lanka, Maldives and Pakistan. President Xi Jinping has commissioned 40 billion dollar maritime silk route and China has been working tirelessly on it. The accelerated speed of Chinese military expenditure has further complicated India's maneuver in the region because the Chinese navy PLAN has been allocated much higher resources in comparison with the Indian navy. The growing imprint of PLAN particularly in South Asia has thrown a series of serious challenges for the Indian navy. Hambantota to Gwadar, China has installed its navy bases across South Asia and it has been perceived by the observers as an effort of China to encircle India within the ambit of maritime in South Asia.[12]

It is important to reformulate maritime policies. Modi government has carried out various exercises and taken many comprehensive steps. We have huge sea coast of over 7400 KM and many islands. Andaman is strategically located and has the potential to contain PLAN moves.

Strengthening of Andaman Command

Modi government has taken many structural steps to contain Chinese navy game plan in the Indian Ocean and elsewhere as well. Strengthening of the Andaman bases has been executed primarily to meet this challenge. Importance of Indian Ocean can be understood from the statement of Admiral A. T. Mahan in 1890 that "Whoever controls the Indian Ocean will dominate Asia. In the 21st century, the destiny of the world would be decided on its waters". Former Prime Minister Shri Atal Bihari Vajpayee also clearly stated India's strategic priorities in November 2003 "the strategic frontiers of today's India, grown in international stature, have expanded well beyond confines of South Asia. Our security environment, ranging from Persian Gulf to Straits of Malacca across the Indian Ocean, includes Central Asia and Afghanistan, China, and South-East Asia. Our strategic thinking has also to extend to these horizons." Hence, Andaman Sea has become a strategic important place to play a major role in maritime security for India. Human civilisations have used Sea extensively for trade and commerce. Due to geographical location of India with the presence of a long coast line provides a huge opportunity in trade and security for its main land. On the other hand presence of ANIs also provide a secure strategy to monitoring the world's most strategic and overcrowded trafficked Malacca Strait, through which approximately 95,000 merchants, oil and gas cargos, pass through.[13] It makes the strait an energy lifeline for Southeast and East Asian countries.

Strait of Malacca is one of the busiest and longest navigation routes which connects the Indian Ocean via Andaman Sea and the Strait is 900 km in length. Besides, this Strait is shortest, safest and economical for ships to travel through East Asia to Europe. Though the Strait is very narrow and with navigational restrictions nevertheless the Strait is still an attractive and preferred navigational route for international shippers compared to other alternative routes like Sunda or Lombok-Makassar Straits in the Indonesian archipelago.[14] Malacca Straits annually provides safe transit to over 60,000 tankers, cargo vessels, passenger vessels, tug and pilot and it is likely to increase in near future. However, Chines goods and oil transportation took place in large volume through Malacca Straits and due to India's territory of Andaman and Nicobar, India is having advantage in the region and any disruptions in the Straits will affect its trade and transit. China is not in a position to deal with such disruption in the Malacca Straits and therefore, China is establishing its bases in different neighbouring countries of India to avoid such scenario.

However, India is a growing economy and its national interest is to promote Act East Policy to counter China in the region as well as initiate development in Northeast region of India. India's long pending development initiative in Northeast region has been initiated by taking up the projects such as the Asian highway project in South Asia to link Singapore with New Delhi via Kuala Lumpur, Ho Chi Minh City, Phnom Penh, Bangkok, Vientiane, Chiang Mai, Yangon, Mandalay, Kalemyo, Tamu, Dhaka and Kolkata. India also has taken initiative to upgrade and resurfacing 160 km long Tamu-Kalewa-Kalemyo road. Besides Kaladan, Multi-modal Transit Transport will connect Indian ports and Sittwe port in Myanmar through Mizoram.[15] It will provide a greater opportunity for the region to develop in every aspect and will provide a huge market for peoples of India and ASEAN as well.

Concluding Remarks

To promote maritime component of "Act East Policy" and strengthen India's strategic interests and regional cooperation with ASEAN, Malacca Strait has to play a dominant role. India has developed the tri-command in Andaman and Nicobar Islands to strengthen its surveillance and monitoring the Malacca Strait as it provides a gateway to the South China Sea and the Pacific Ocean. Majority of Chinese oil supply ships from the Middle East still passes through this narrow way, which is a nightmare for the Chinese due to its proximity with the Andaman. India has already upgraded maritime relations with the Indo-Pacific countries and pledged to further accelerate the process. Maritime power is extremely important to sustain the dominance of a country. ASEAN countries wish India to play a counter balancing role against China in the region. Following comment of Jakarta Times vindicates this point:

> "The evolving geo-strategic framework inexorably impels countries in South East Asia to accept China and India as major regional powers. In the first case, it is necessary consequence of the former.... Beijing has also shown an unequalled zest in its economic diplomacy with the association of South East Asian nations, ASEAN. Delhi on the other hand has been a late bloomer...ASEAN wants India's presence as much as India needs to be active in the region....ASEAN makes available a strategic framework and regulated forum which India can bluntly interact with economic powers Japan and South Korea along with fellow regional power China. This is an opportunity in which Delhi must not be hesitant. It cannot afford to miss the boat again."[16]

Australia-India relations have also improved particularly in the backdrop of November 2014. It was maiden Indian PM visit after three decades which has accelerated the pace of deepening of bilateral relationship. Australia is India's maritime neighbour and our deepening bonhomie has saddened China. India has been engaged in joint maritime exercises with coincidently democratic countries (Japan, United States, Australia and many ASEAN countries). This has created apprehensions in Chinese strategist thinkers. China's naval watchers have in particular been suspicious of naval exercises involving India, Japan, Australia and the United States, ostensibly aimed at balancing Chinese maritime power in the Asian littorals.[17]

The return of PM Modi for the second term in May 2019 has further given new momentum to India's maritime policy. It remains bedrock of India's Act East Policy. It requires gamut of changes and more resources are required to meet with the swelling expenditure of our navy. Modi government has taken many positive steps in this direction and realignment with the like-minded countries has further consolidated our status in larger context of the Indo-Pacific region.

Notes

1 Griffiths, Martin & Terry O Callaghan, *Key Concepts in International Relations,* Routledge, London, 2004, P-13.

2 Herz, John, H, Idealist Internationalism and Security Dilemma, *World Politics,* Volume-2, 1950,P-157-158.

3 Dasgupta, Saibal, China sees growing India-Japan ties as move to counter it, *Times of India,* New Delhi, September 20, 2012.

4 Ibid

5 Daniel Rajendran, India's New Asia-Pacific Strategy, *The Lowy Institute,* December 2014.

6 Scott Cheney Peters , India's Maritime Acts in the East, *Asia Maritime Transparency Initiative,* June 18, 2015.

7 *Richard Heydarian,* Why China's 'militiasation' of the South China Sea needs a review by the Philippines-US alliance, *South China Post International,* Hongkong, July 22, 2019.

8 Ministry of Defence, Government of India, Annual Reports,

9 *Times of India,* New Delhi, June 9, 2017.

10 *The Hindu,* New Delhi, January 16, 2016.

11 Vishal Ranjan, Australia and India in Asia, 'Look West meets Act East' *Strategic Analysis,* IDSA, Volume-40, 2016.

12 Arun Prakash, A Strategic Encirclement, *Indian Express,* New Delhi, 25 April 2017.

13 Sudhir Devare, *India & Southeast Asia: Towards Security Convergence* (Singapore: Institute of Southeast Asian Studies, 2006).

14 Sam Bateman, Catherine Zara Raymond and Joshua Ho, "Safety and Security in Malacca & Singapore Straits", Policy Paper, *Maritime Security Programme,* Institute of Defence & Strategic Studies, Singapore, 2006.

15 Available at https://www.security-risks.com/ (accessed on 10th April 2019)

16 "Is India Ready to be part of South East Asia Again?", Editorial, *Jakarta Post,* Jakarta, June 18, 2007.

17 'Australia woes India to Counter balance China' , *The Global Times,* July 27, 2017.

Maritime Security: Global Repercussions of Emerging Terror Threats in Indian Ocean Region

Aswani R.S.

International relations is mostly deliberated as a conflict-based paradigm in which the main actors are nation-states for whom power and security become the central issues, and in which there is hardly any value for morality. Fear and lack of trust become the basis of all actions and it contributes to an underlying presence of security dilemma in all the actvities of nation states. Indian Ocean Region (IOR) also projects a security dilemma that has created complex polictical relations. The Indian Ocean Region has turned into a center of global power conflicts in the 21st century mainly due to the impending war between India and China for dominance in these warm waters and due to the fluid political scenario in the Middle East and the surging value of Persian oil in the global market. Bouchard & Crumplin (2010), added to these variants the renewed interests of a new triangular play, 'American's heavy military interventionism, China's arrival on the regional chessboard and the rise of India as a real Indian Ocean great power.' Thus, the 21st century has seen a strategic reassessment of the global geopolitical significance of IOR (Rumley, Doyle , & Chaturvedi, 2012).

The excessive foreign intervention in the local political scenario in IOR is likewise considered as one of the crucial elements that has augmented the political conflicts in this region, with a record of nearly 46.6 percent of all the recorded conflicts worldwide in IOR alone (Bouchard & Crumplin, 2010). Weak state capacity is cited as one of the prominent reasons for such interference of foreign powers in IOR, which has fueled the resource scarcity and socio-political tensions in this region (Bouchard & Crumplin, 2010).Indian Ocean has thus becomes world's most important energy and trade maritime route. The strategic rivalry in the Indian Ocean can no longer be neglected, nor can Indian Ocean geopolitics. This region has become the nexus of food and energy security not only for the 56 littoral countries on the region, but also for Far East and for Far Western countries. It occupies the lifeline of largely populated countries such as China and India, connecting them to the Middle East for oil and gas. The small island nations in the region also are critical to the security of the region, as their political inclinations directly influence peace and order in IOR. The global strategic and military interests are pursued by all major countries in the globe either directly or indirectly in IOR. After the British withdrawal by 1960s from the IOR, it has again become leading strategic theatre for global trade and commerce. Surrounded by unstable, poor, populated countries, the region has gained the global attention for resource conflicts and boundary disputes. Thus, this centuries long, neglected region of the globe, has already occupied the center stage for all the opportunities and vulnerabilities of global geo politics.

In the preponderance of these military security threats in the popular narratives of international politics, the major non-traditional ones are not adequately studied. Hence, this chapter attempts to study the non-state factors that precariously affect the order in IOR. They are generally classified as non-traditional in nature. Non-traditional, non-state security threats are those concerns that rise mainly from non-mainstream institutions and which pose challenges to the existence and security of states and people. This notion of a new maritime security narrative is transformative and has advanced from a traditional, narrowed impression of naval power projections from a nation-state perspective to an interdisciplinary study that encompasses new emerging discourses such as environmentalism, climate change etc. However, this chapter studies the military terror threats of the Indian Ocean that arises from non-state actors, such as terror organizations that work in parallel to nation-states.

Maritime Terrorism

Maritime Terrorism is a growing threat to the world, which has the potentiality to uproot the trade dynamics of Indian Ocean. Oceans are a large entity and its extensive shores are constantly unmonitored, which creates an environment of a constant threat of terror. Maritime terror activities can be defined as, 'any illegal activities directed against ships, their passengers, cargo or crew, or against seaports with the intent of directly or indirectly influencing a government or group of individuals' (Invalid source specified). Maritime terrorist activities include smuggling of drugs, trafficking of people, and illegal transportation of arms and weapons of mass destruction. However, high intensity maritime terrorist activities include direct attacks on ships or ports and hijackings of ships. The terrorism that is rampant in the land has transverse to the sea, overlapping conventional boundaries, failing the past inadequate and incongruous counter proliferation policies (Asal & Rethemeyer, 2008).

The Al-Qaeda planned and executed the terrorist attack on USS Cole in 2000, while bunkering at the Aden port. This is labelled as the most noxious attack on a naval ship, in the 21st century (Walker, 2012). The attack was suicidal in nature, adding to the risks of the Sea Lines of Communication in the Indian Ocean. The port security even transcends from mere focus on land to water, nonetheless the boundlessness of the sea makes monitoring a tedious task. The suicide boat bombing of MV Limburg in 2002, a Crude Oil Carrier registered under the French flag was another instance of maritime terrorism in the Indian Ocean. MV Limburg was a commercial ship and the attack on it caused Yemen millions of revenue loss (Henley & Stewart, 2002). As a result, Aden and the Persian Gulf came under the ambit of unsafe SLOCS, highlighting the possible damage to human and material resources in the Indian Ocean, due to maritime terrorism. The latest attack by the Filipino Abu Sayyaf extremists, on the Vietnam cargo ship (Singh, 2017), depicts the proximity of maritime terrorism in Indian Ocean Region to the world's busiest maritime routes.

These direct terrorist attacks on maritime property could quickly spread to the ports, killing more people and causing more damages, if not curtailed diligently. The naval capabilities of the terrorist organizations such as ISIS, Al-Qaeda, etc. are increasing multifold, in competitive capability with the prominent national navies (Asal & Hastings, 2014). E.g., the erstwhile LTTE operated a naval fleet, much superior in capacity to the Sri Lankan national navy. Thus, national navies independently would be unable to tackle this enormous issue. The vastness of the coasts and its inability to be unmanned increases such terror possibilities and thus require a grand initiative of all countries in the world to join hands.

The land is on the constant watch of a sovereign government, unlike the vast expanses of an ocean, which has overlapping claims by neighboring states and those who rightfully use it for their trade and transit (Das, 2018). This makes strict compliance to national security, a challenging scheme. India has faced a high-intensity maritime security breach or an incident of maritime terrorism during 26/11 attacks of Mumbai. This 2008 Mumbai attack is considered a violation of India's coastal security and hence, after this incident, the coastal security has been tightened and made rigid. Indian Government diverted considerable funds to increase the capacity of the Indian Coast Guards through personnel induction and addition of ships and weaponry. Thus, the surveillance of the Indian coasts has become stringent, and India has entered into agreements with its neighbors and other prominent powers who have their presence in IOR to crash any such attempts of maritime terrorism. Such a nexus between coastal nations in IOR is obligatory for ensuring the coastal security of all the nations in the region in particular and the global maritime region in general.

Nincic (2007) opines that the future of maritime security is bleak as terrorist organizations have floated to the sea and have started using merchant ships as a means of transporting and spreading terror. Similar to the use of cars and airplanes (9/11 attacks), Nincic predicts that the ships will be the future 'weaponized transportation' (Invalid source specified). He proposes two ways of using the ships: one as a means of proliferation- to spread through transportation or the other is the ships themselves as weapons of mass destruction. It would be similar to the suicide bombing that happened using flights in the USA. Any such ships would be used to blast open nuclear or chemical weaponry near a thickly populated city and thus, could contribute to the doom of a nation. Just as merchant ships are capable of transporting high magnitude of goods and services, they are capable of shipping massive heaps of terror too.

Maritime Piracy

Maritime Piracy is considered as deliberated crimes at sea, which happen for monetary advantage. It is not targeted at any particular nation and is driven by a universal hatred, which makes it difficult to curb the pirate attacks. Though it is popularly shown heroic in many Hollywood movies to be a Pirate, the harshness of the sea, the economic conditions of those who turn into pirates and the death toll are massive. Pirate attacks happen in high frequency across the globe, and the Indian Ocean is undoubtedly a high-intensity pirate attack prone region. Hundreds of ships and thousands of crew members are attacked and held hostage, every year for heavy ransom and sometimes, it even leads to the murder of the ship crew. The major pirate attack prone zones of the world are in the Indian Ocean, including Malacca Strait and Singapore Strait in the Bay of Bengal, South China Sea, Somalian Coasts near Africa, and Suez Canal near the Middle East, etc.

In 2015, there were 50 pirate attacks in the Singapore Strait alone and around 30 in Malacca Strait, which is the busiest maritime route in the world. In the recent times, maritime piracy resulted in a dramatic increase in maritime theft, hijacking, and violence due to the advance in technology and development in the approaches towards crime. The targets of pirates are cargo and transport ships and most times; innocent fishers become victims of such cold-blooded murder at sea.

Piracy undoubtedly has become the significant threat of 21st century maritime affairs, which needs to be addressed at the earliest by all the countries in the world. Individual nations cannot address these issues, as the sea is a massive expanse and piracy a much considerable concern. Pirate kingpins, their intermediaries and ransom negotiators rule the sea in the Indian Ocean. There is very little government presence in shipping villages and coastal towns of Somalia. Poverty and unemployment are two major factors for the increase in piracy as frustrated by hunger and poor living conditions, and more youth are pushed into this shady career as an opportunity to make quick money and to uplift their families from the dungeons.

Piracy has cost 62 deaths out of the 3500 captives in the Indian Ocean alone (Reuters, 2016) and it is causing a considerable loss to the shipping sector of the world. Increasing patrolling and armed presence of naval forces across the Indian Ocean is one solution that is currently followed. The single thrust of world navies, increase the pressure on pirates and thus they could be reluctant from attacking the commercial and passenger ships traversing the seas. However, this is only a partial solution and does not remove the problem from its roots. To resolve this issue permanently, the Somalian Government has to be strengthened multi-folded. The self-sufficiency of the Somalian Government increases their capability to provide opportunities for financial growth to the youth there, which advances their living standards and keep them away from entering into criminal activities. It also provides security to their lives and their families. Such a socio-economic order is desirable in Somalia to ward off piracy, and it could happen only with the support of world governments.

International Maritime Safety Mechanisms

The safety of Sea Lines of Communication is a major concern for the shipping companies, littoral nations and the International Maritime Organization (IMO). To ensure the twin objectives of *safer ships and cleaner oceans*, IMO has introduced the International Ship and Port Facility Security (ISPS) in the year 2004(Daud, 2014). Every ship needs to comply with the safety management codes mentioned in ISPS and the ports are advised to follow the safety instructions too. ISPS targets for early detection of maritime security threats and provides a detailed mechanism of terror prevention and mitigation. It includes three classification of maritime security (MARSEC Levels) at ports (Balog, 2002). The first level is a normal one, when every ship and port handle day-to-day affairs with adequate care and alertness. The second level is a heightened one, when there is an obvious threat to the port, some additional security measures will be implemented. The third level is the elevated one when there is a certain attack being predicted or anticipated, but the information is inadequate.

The SUA Convention (Convention for the Suppression of Unlawful Acts against the Safety of Maritime Navigation) has been in vogue since the previous decade and it intends to ensure that no- unauthorized personnel get on board the ships, in between departure and arrival and thus, create a safe and supervised navigation. It also warrants that the ships not be used for any unlawful activities that hinders the safety of sea lines (IMO, 2005).

Customs–Trade Partnership against Terrorism (C-TPAT) is an intended association of governments and trade companies, in order to conduct risk-assessment and terrorism prevention. Information is exchanged through C-TPAT, across borders in order to tackle the issues of maritime terrorism. Without such wholehearted cooperation of participatory nations, terrorism in the oceans cannot be controlled. The monetary loss of cargo and ship runs to millions and the loss of human lives to this forbidding terror is inexplicable. C-TPAT follows a voluntary mechanism of supply- chain security assurance (Mento, 2004) and hence, the cooperation of governments and businesses are sought to arrive at policy suggestions, which could ensure the safety of sea lines of communication in the Indian Ocean.

Conclusion

Security is a complex phenomenon and the scale and range of challenges in 21st century makes it even harder for concerned parties to ensure stability in their neighborhood. Peace and security becomes a shared responsibility of all the littoral nations and other players in the Indian Ocean. There is no doubt about the fact that Indian Ocean has turned into the hotbed of global politics. The criticality of Sea lines of communication and the need to protect the global commons has brought in extra regional players and has contributed to tensions in the areas of interest(Vasan , 2012).Indian Ocean has opened its vulnerable borders to inculcate many novel concerns like global terrorism, piracy, environmental issues, manmade and natural disasters etc. Indian Ocean was decided to be nurtured as a zone of peace since 1971 after many deliberations, and due to many geo-political concerns; it stays as a dream farther away. The stability and security of the Indian Ocean Region concerns not only the littoral nations sharing the sea borders alone but also the 'user' nations whose ships ply the ocean with oil and other essential supplies.

Thus, there exists a security dilemma in IOR that has pre-occupied all the regional countries and major international players, that the major issues of terror in the region are neglected. Indian Ocean witness multitudes of naval exercises by both regional and extra regional powers and the threat of force or terror attacks have added to the apprehensions of the littoral states. There is thus an augmenting need for effective legal farmework internationally to implement the existing security laws and also there ought to be futuristic measures for capacity-building and cooperation among the littoral states. Fears and apprehensions related to the potential impacts of measures to improve maritime security also require attention along with the revival of a rich maritme heritage. There needs to be an institutionalised efforts to coordinate the Indian Ocean maritime security system. It is vital to the security and safety of all littoral states along with the ships that pass through these arteries of world trade.Such institutionalisations have to take direct and indirect measures to coordiante governments and non-governmental organisations and mostly people to people exchanges for better confidence building measures and continued vigilance.

References

Asal , V., & Hastings, J. V. (2014, September 16). *Terror at Sea: Exploring Maritime Targeting by Terrorist Organizations.* Retrieved from piracy studies.org: http://piracy-studies.org/terror-at-sea-exploring-maritime-targeting-by-terrorist-organizations/

Balog, J. (2002). *Public Transportation Security.* Transportation Research Board.

Bouchard , C., & Crumplin, W. (2010, June 1). Neglected no longer: the Indian Ocean at the forefront of world geopolitics and global geostrategy. *Journal of the Indian Ocean Region.*

Das, P. (2018, July-August). Why Do Terror Groups Choose Coastal Routes To Strike? *India Foundation Journal.*

Daud, R. (2014). *The Impacts of International Ship and Port Facility Security (ISPS) Code on Port User at Port of Tanjung Pelepas.* Malaysia: Universiti Utara Malaysia. College of Law, Government, and International Studies.

Harman, S. (2016). *Confidence-building measure.* Encyclopædia Britannica, inc. Retrieved from https://www.britannica.com/topic/confidence-building-measure

Henley , J., & Stewart, H. (2002, October 7). Al-Qaida suspected in tanker explosion. *The Guardian.* Retrieved from https://www.theguardian.com/world/2002/oct/07/alqaida.france

Mento, P. (2004). *C-TPAT and ISA, Understanding the Effectiveness of Trade Partnerships for Customs Enforcement.* North Carolina: Lulu.com.

Raghavan, V., & Prabhakaran, L. W. (2008). *Maritime Security in the Indian Ocean Region: Critical Issues in Debate.* New York: Tata McGraw-Hill Publishing Company.

Roe, P. (1999, March). The Intrastate Security Dilemma: Ethnic Conflict as a 'Tragedy'? *Journal of Peace Research, 36*(2), 183–202.

Rumley, D., Doyle , T., & Chaturvedi, S. (2012, April). Securing' the Indian Ocean? Competing Regional Security Constructions. April 2012). *Journal of the Indian Ocean, 8.*

Singh, A. (2017, March 3). The changing face of maritime terrorism. *The Strategist .*

Spykman, N. (1938). Geography and Foreign Policy, II. *American Political Science Review, 32,* 236.

Vasan , R. (2012). Maritime Security and Challenges in the Indian Ocean Region. *South Asia Analysis .*

Walker, A. (2012, June 5). Breaking The Bottleneck: Maritime Terrorism and "Economic Chokepoints". *Nato Association.* Retrieved from http://natoassociation.ca/breaking-the-bottleneck-maritime-terrorism-and-economic-chokepoints-part-1/

Features of Indian Coastal Area in the backdrop of Coastal Security

Dr P.S. Swathi Lekshmi

The Republic of India has nine coastal States and four Union Territories. It is blessed with a long coast line of 7,517 Km, of which 5,422 kms lie in the mainland and the rest is distributed on the islands in the nine States and four Union Territories. The coastal Union Territories which are island areas being Andaman and Nicobar and the Lakshadweep islands, the former with a coastline of 132 km and the latter with a coastline of 1,962 km. The highly indented coastline of the country makes it vulnerable to security threats and infiltration by terrorist and militant attack in addition to other threats such as smuggling and carrying of arms and ammunition.

It is estimated that 95 percent of India's trade by volume and 70 percent by value is done through maritime transport. This assumes strategic importance more so because India sits centrally at the cross roads of Trans Indian Ocean Routes. The cargo ships sailing between East Asia, America, Europe and Africa pass through Indian Territorial waters. Added to this, there has been an unsettled and disputed nature of some of India's maritime boundaries.

India shares 14,880 km of boundary with Pakistan, China, Nepal, Bhutan, Myanmar and Bangladesh (Das, 2010). Including a small segment with Afghanistan (106 km) in northern Jammu and Kashmir (J&K), now part of the Northern Areas of Pakistan Occupied Kashmir (POK), India's land borders exceed 15,000 km shared with seven countries. (Kanwal, 2007). The coastline of peninsular India is bordered by the Bay of Bengal in the east, the Indian Ocean in the south and the Arabian sea in the west. India shares its maritime boundaries with seven countries namely, Pakistan, the Maldives, Sri Lanka, Indonesia, Thailand, Myanmar and Bangladesh (Roy-Chaudhury, 2005).

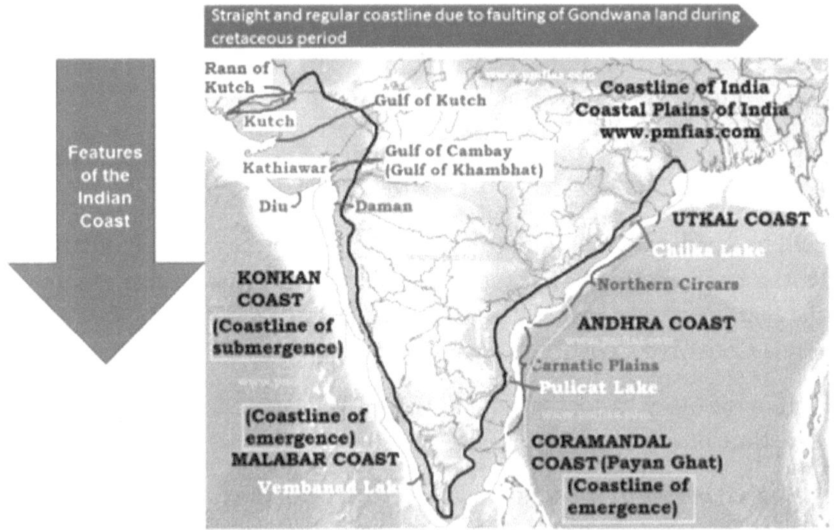

Along the East coast of India, the coasts are known by specific names such as along Odisha coast, it is known as Utkal Coast, and from the southern limit of the Utkal plain starts the Andhra Coast, and the south of the Andhra plain lies the Tamil Nadu Coast. The Tamil Nadu coast and parts of Andhra coast together are known as Coramandal Coast or Payan Ghat. The west coast strip extends from the Gulf of Cambay (Gulf of Khambhat) in the north to Cape Comorin (Kanniyakumari). Starting from north to south, it is divided into (i) the Konkan coast, (ii) the Karnataka coast and (iii) the Kerala coast.

It is made up of alluvium brought down by the short streams originating from the Western Ghats.

It is dotted with a large number of coves (a very small bay), creeks (a narrow, sheltered waterway such as an inlet in a shoreline or channel in a marsh) and a few estuaries. (Marine Landforms).

Thus the Konkan coast consists of the Maharashtra coast and Goa coast, the Malabar Coast consists of Karnataka and Kerala coasts. Along the west coast, the Konkan coast is called as the coastline of submergence and the Malabar Coast, coastline of emergence. Coastline of emergence is formed either by an uplift of the land or by the lowering of the sea level. Coastline of submergence is an exact opposite case. Bars, spits, lagoons, salt marshes, beaches, sea cliffs and arches are the typical features of emergence. (Marine Landforms)

The east coast of India, especially its south-eastern part (Tamil Nadu coast), appears to be a coast of emergence.

The west coast of India, on the other hand, is both emergent and submergent.

The northern portion of the coast is submerged as a result of faulting and the southern portion, that is the Kerala coast, is an example of an emergent coast. Coramandal coast (Tamil Nadu) and the Malabar Coast (Kerala Coast)is a Coastline of emergence.

On the other hand, the Konkan coast (Maharashtra and Goa Coast) is a Coastline of submergence.

Given below, in the following table are the differences with respect to Physical features between the East coast and the West coast as well as the differences from a fisheries perspective.

Differences between the East Coast and West Coast

Physical Features	East Coast	West Coast
	Lies between Eastern Ghats and the Bay of Bengal and extends from Ganga delta to Kanyakumari.	Extends from Gulf of Cambay in the north to Cape Comorin in the South.
	The predominant lagoon systems of the east coast are Chilka lake and Pulicat lake.	Konkan (Maharashtra and Goa) Karnataka, Malabar and Kerala Coast
	Marked by deltas formed by	
Differences from a Fisheries point of view		
Fish landings	30 % of fish landings take place.	70% of fish landings take place.
Continental shelf	Narrow and its width varies from 80-180 km.	Broad and its width varies from 50-340 km.

Physical Features	East Coast	West Coast
State of sea	More turbulent due to frequent weather conditions/weather systems	Less turbulent except during south west monsoon.
Phytoplankton production	Low production compared to west coast (November-December maximum production) and June-September is the secondary peak.	High production compared to East Coast (June-September maximum production, November–December, secondary peak.)
Temperature fluctuation	Fluctuations are less between 27 and 29 Degree Celsius.	Fluctuations are more ranging between 23 and 29 Degree Celsius.
Upwelling	Not common but reported to occur.	Common during monsoon and post monsoon season.(May-November)
Salinity	Lower (30-34 ppt)	Higher (34-37 ppt)
Nutrients	High concentration not present.	High concentration present during upwelling.

Coastal Resources of India:

The following are the coastal resources of the country.

Length of coastline	7517 km
Exclusive Economic zone	2.02 million sq. km
Continental shelf	0.506 million sq.km
Rivers and canals	1.96 lakh km stretch
Reservoirs	29.07 lakh hectares
Ponds and tanks	24.40 lakh ha
Beels and Derelict waters	7.98 lakh ha
Brackish waters	12.40 lakh ha

India is thus blessed with an abundance of water bodies along its coastline as well as hinterland and the land borders consist of undulated and ragged terrains, marshy lands, evergreen jungles, deserts and snow covered peaks which provide the perfect cover for terrorist infiltration either through land border or sea, aids in smuggling of arms, ammunition, narcotics, drugs and other contraband consignments which offer vantage points for such dreaded activities.

Major Issues from the point of Maritime Security

Cross Border Terrorism with Pakistan

The Radcliffe line which defined the Indo-Pakistan border and which was formed in 1947, defines the areas bordering the erstwhile states of Jammu and Kashmir (presently, the Union territories of Jammu and Kashmir and the Union territory of Ladakh), Gujarat, Punjab and Rajasthan. The main challenges encountered along this border are infiltration and smuggling. Along the border of India and Pakistan lies Sir Creek estuary, which is a 96 km tidal estuary and the dispute arises between the claim on the borderline by India and Pakistan. The first verdict regarding the claim was reached in 1968 wherein, Pakistan was awarded 10 % of its claim along the 9,100 sq km and India, 90% of its claim along the border. There has been 12 rounds of talks since 1969 with no major breakthrough and in 2012, India proposed that the maritime boundary should be demarcated as per the technical provisions of the International Law of the Sea which Pakistan had staunchly refused. Pakistan has said that an international arbitration should be called for, for which India has not agreed since it wants the bilateral disputes to be resolved without the intervention of a third party.

Indo Sri Lankan Border dispute:

This issue deserves strategic importance since, the bone of contention between the two countries arises mainly due to the claim for fisheries resources. Palk Bay is a strip of water that separated India and Sri Lanka. This Bay defines the International maritime boundary across the two countries. The Palk Strait is 22 miles of water expanse and separates the northern coast of Sri Lanka from the south east coast of India. The maritime agreements between the two countries were started in 1974 and 1976 which adversely affected the livelihoods of thousands of Indian fishermen. The Indian fishermen were not willing to give up the privileges of fishing rights across the maritime border which they had enjoyed for centuries. The magnetic pull exerted by the rich prawn resources on which existed on the other side of the Indo Sri Lankan maritime boundary, on the Indian fishermen often led to the latter being caught and seized with their men and materials and fishing boats, fired at, intimidated or imprisoned.

There are also frequent reports of Sri Lankan fishermen infringing in to Indian waters and resorting to illegal fishing activities mostly involving in multiday fishing, off the coast of Tamil Nadu, Andhra Pradesh, Kerala and the Andaman and Nicobar Islands.

Indo-Bangladesh border dispute

Along the India Bangladesh border lies the New Moore island which is mainly uninhabited but both countries laid claim to this because of the abundance of oil and natural gases in this region. In 2014, by virtue of the United Nations tribunal, nearly four fifth of the 25,000 sqkm of the exclusive economic zone was demarcated for Bangladesh. The verdict, binding on both countries, opens the way for Bangladesh to explore for oil and gas in the Bay of Bengal, and ends a dispute over a sea border with India that has disrupted ties between the neighbors thus putting an end to the 40 year old maritime dispute between both the countries.

Role of Indian Fishermen in maintaining Coastal Security:

➢ Concepts of Territorial waters, EEZ, Continental Shelf came in to existence in 1976 following the UNCLOS meeting in 1973.

➢ Indian Coast Guard (ICG) was established in 1977, under Ministry of Defense (Surveillance from shoreline to 12 nm) along with marine police, beyond 50nm by Indian Navy.

➢ Fishermen groups designated as *"Sagar Suraksha Dal"* participate along with ICG for monitoring sea and coastal waters and for reporting suspicious activities.

➢ Marine police have formed *"Gram Raksha Dal" (Respectable village elders)*

➢ Indian navy and ICG conduct periodic community interaction programmes for raising awareness among fishing communities regarding the importance of up keeping coastal security.

Review of Coastal Security Mechanism in India:

➢ Vessels of coastal States are registered under uniform registration system for different color codes for fishing trawlers of different States.

➢ Fishing trawlers 20 mts and above to be fitted with type B transponder.

- ➤ Smaller vessels have Radio Frequency Identification Device (RFID).

- ➤ Distress Alert Transmitters (DAT) to alert Coast Guard at times of distress.

- ➤ Coastal security helpline nos 1554 (Coast guard) and 1093 (Marine Police) given to fishermen.

- ➤ Biometric data to identify fishermen at sea through issue of I.D Cards *(fed into centralised data base)*.

Coastal Surveillance Network Project:

- ➤ Real time surveillance up to 25 nm in to sea

- ➤ Setting up of 46 static radars along coastline

- ➤ National Automatic Identification System (NAIS) to track and monitor vessels by receiving feeds from AIS transponders in sailing vessels

- ➤ Vessel Traffic Management System (VTMS) Installed in all major ports

- ➤ Fishermen offer to be sentinels of the Indian Coast *(Mail Online,July 21,2016)*

References:

Kanwal, (2007) Gurmeet Kanwal "India's Borders"; *Unending Threats and Challenges*, 23(1), http//www.indiadefence review.com/2008/10indias-borders.html. (25-05-2009)

Roy Chaudhury, (2005) Sea Power and Indian Security.Brasseys First Edition.

Suresh R, (2014) Maritime Security of India: The Coastal Security Challenges and Policy Options (Ed.) Vij Books India Pvt. Ltd. New Delhi 2014 ISBN:9789382652366

Suresh R, (2015) The Changing Dimensions of Security: India's Security Policy Options, (Ed.) Vij Books India Pvt. Ltd. New Delhi, ISBN: 978-93-84464-80-6

Suresh R & Rakhee Viswambharan, (2014) Coastal Security of India: The Role of Coastal Community in Maritime Security of India: The Coastal Security Challenges and Policy Options (Ed.) Vij Books India Pvt. Ltd. New Delhi 2014 ISBN:9789382652366

The Role of Coastal Community in Coastal Security: A Descriptive Study

Rakhee Viswambharan

Introduction

In the post-cold war period the threat to the security of nation states emanates mainly from non-state actors. Unlike the attack from state actors the non-state actors mode of attack is different. It demands a constant vigil throughout the land and maritime borders. Coastal security is one of the subsets of maritime security. The coastal security has become an urgent necessity especially in the context of the 2008 Mumbai terrorist attack and the threat it poses to the national security. The 2012 Italian marine issue have added a new dimension to the security of the coastal people engaged in fishing.

When we look into the coastal security a convergence of the national security concerns and human security concerns is visible. The overall development of the coastal area would lead to better human security and better human security would result in enlisting the support of the coastal community to ensure national security programme, especially the coastal security. However the task of guarding the vast coastline, unlike our land borders, is a complex issue involving multiple stake holders such as shipping, fisheries, offshore exploration and production, tourism, and scientific community. In short, coastal security is not only about protecting our coastal terrain and territorial waters from direct attacks from state actors or non-state actors, but also safeguarding the interests of all stake holders.

Coastal States/Union Territories in India and the Length of Coastal Area

Sl.No.	State/Union Territory	Length (in km.)
1.	Gujarat	1214.70
2.	Maharashtra	652.60
3.	Goa	101.00
4.	Karnataka	208.00
5.	Kerala	569.70
6.	Tamil Nadu	906.90
7.	Andhra Pradesh	973.70
8.	Odisha	476.70
9.	West Bengal	157.50
10.	Daman & Diu	42.50
11.	Puducherry	47.60
12.	Lakshadweep	132.00
13.	Andaman & Nicobar Islands	1962.00
	TOTAL	7516.60

Source: Annual Report 2017-2018, Ministry of Home Affairs, GOI.

Basic Features of Coastal India

India's mainland coast extends to 5500 km and Islands to 2016.60 kms bringing it to a total of 7516.60 kms including the Andaman & Nicobar (A&N) and Lakshadweep Islands. And nearly 25 per cent of the India's population is living within 50 km of the coast. A wide range of coastal ecologically sensitive areas such as mangroves, sea grass, coral reefs, tidal flats, estuaries, lagoons, sand dunes and salt marshes occur along the coast. A number of rivers flow into the Bay of Bengal on the east coast and into the Arabian Sea on the west coast, carrying large quantities of sediment. The east coast is dominated by large river deltas and sandy beaches, while the westcoast consists of an intricate network of estuaries, backwaters and predominantly rocky coastline. The coastal habitats alone account for approximately one-third of all marine biological productivity and estuarine ecosystems (salt marshes, sea grasses, mangrove forests) are among the most productive regions. The coastal ecologically sensitive areas are home to unique flora and fauna. The coral reefs constitute less than 1 per cent of the ocean floor but support over 25 per cent of the marine biodiversity. The mangroves, beaches and coral reefs support in controlling coastal erosion, shoreline change and also serve as a natural defense against coastal hazards such as storm surges, cyclones and tsunamis.

Major Issues along the Indian Coast

1. Destruction of coastal ecosystems;

2. Vulnerability to cyclones and storm surges;

3. Sea erosion;

4. Pollution caused by industries, sewage discharge;

5. Overpopulation;

6. Food insecurity;

7. Scarcity of freshwater supply due to salt water intrusion;

8. Lack of infrastructural development such as roads, educational institutions, markets, health centres, recreations.

Coastal Community in India

The survey carried out along the Indian coastal area reveals that except in Gujarat the coastal community in other coastal states is living in abject poverty. There are many causes for the poverty especially among the coastal community engaged in traditional fishing. This includes, the uncertainty in the traditional fish catching and also due to the mechanized fishing by trawlers and other deep sea fishing methods. They are also facing problem related to adverse climate conditions. The daily income of some of the traditional fisherman is very low compared to their counter parts working in other areas, including agriculture. The risk factor is also very much in fishing and related activities. They are the victims of natural calamities. As far as the supports from the governmental agencies are concerned they seldom receive the benefits of the programme meant for their welfare. Most of these benefits never reach them mainly due to the bureaucratic corruption. Secondly, the government policy formulations they were not represented. Therefore most of the policy initiative for their welfare is not in tune with their requirements. The absence of an institutional mechanism to aggregate and articulate their aspirations and requirements is well visible along the coastal area. In this regard their position in the existing system of administration is similar to that of the Scheduled Tribes and Scheduled Castes. (SureshR)

Fishers in the Coastal India

The CMFRI census data 2010 shows that there are nearly 61 per cent of fishermen families come under Below Poverty Line (BPL). Almost 58 per cent of the fisher folk were educated with different levels of education. About 38 per cent of marine fisher folk were engaged in active fishing with 85 per cent of them having full time engagement. About 63.6 per cent of the fisher folk were engaged in fishing and allied activities. Among the marine fishermen households nearly 76 per cent were Hindus, 15 per cent were Christians and 9 per cent were Muslims. Among the marine fishermen households 131,012 families were having lifesaving equipment. In the marine fisheries sector, there were 194,490 crafts in the fishery out of which 37 per cent were mechanized, 37 per cent were motorized and 26 per cent were non-motorized. Out of a total of 167,957 crafts fully owned by fisher folk, 53 per cent were non-motorized, 24 per cent were motorized and 23 per cent were mechanized. Among the mechanized crafts fully owned by fishermen, 29 per cent were trawlers, 43 per cent were gillneters and 19 per cent were dolnetters. (CMFRI Census)

Economic Status

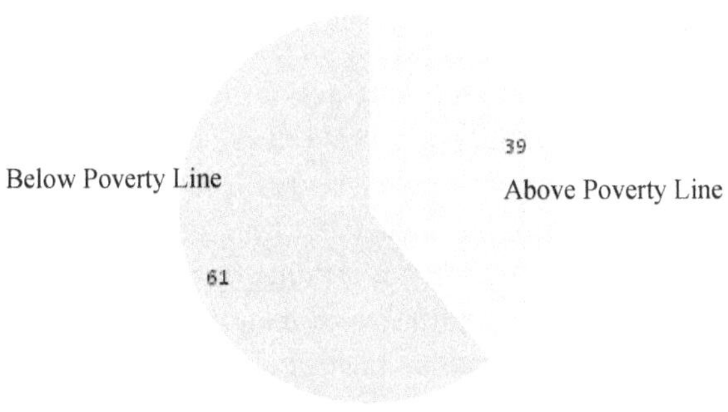

Educational Standard

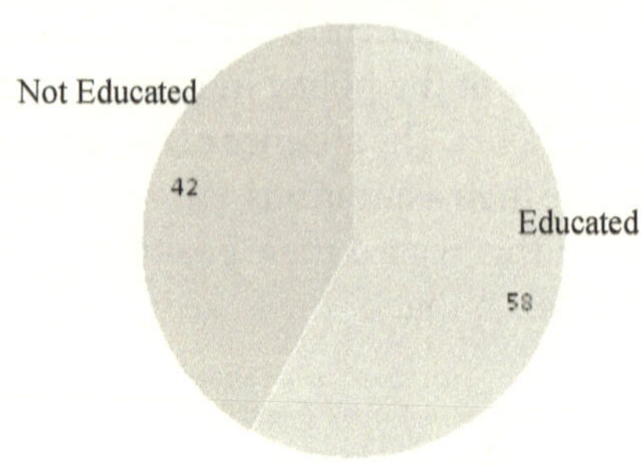

It is also found that among the marine fishermen households 131,012 families were having lifesaving equipment. There were 18,539 fishermen households owning GPS which was used while fishing. Among the fisher folks 279,239 households were having mobile phones for communication. There are 26,351 families are having other lifesaving gadgets in their possession. Out of a total of 167,957 crafts owned by fisher folks 52.6 per cent were non- motorized and 23.1 per cent mechanized. Among the motorized crafts owned by fisher folk 60.3 percent were fiber glass boats, 12.5 percent plywood boat, 10.3 percent plank built boats and 8.9 per cent were catamaran. (CMFRI Census)

The coastal community faces multifarious problem. These problems can be broadly classified as livelihood problem and the security problem. They are not getting a better livelihood from their fishing activity. This is mainly due to the uncertainty prevalent in the traditional fishing sector. The daily income from fish catch varies according to seasons. This uncertainty in income further lead the fisher folk to borrowing money from private moneylenders, who charge exorbitant interest rates and put them in debt trap. Though the cooperative sectors are active along the coastal area, they failed to cater to the needs of the coastal community. Therefore, the rural banking sector needs to be strengthened along the coastal area. In this connection the financial inclusion schemes of the Union government like, Jan Dhan Yojana along the coastal region also need special attention. During the field survey carried out along the coastal area it is revealed that most of the fisher community is not even aware of the centrally sponsored financial inclusion programme. The indifferent attitude of bureaucracy working in the coastal area and also lack of initiative from nongovernmental agencies had augmented the problem of financial inclusion of the fisherfolk. The voluntary agencies and also the self-help groups can address this issue very effectively. The educational institutions located in the coastal area can play a leading role in creating awareness among the fishers regarding the financial inclusion programme. Again the local self- government institutions can also involve in the awareness programme on financial inclusion. If the community orientation programmes of the security agencies are effective and periodic, the coastal police can also create awareness among the coastal community on the various schemes of the governmental agencies for the fishers welfare and empowerment.[37]

In order to ascertain the daily income of the coastal community the fishers were asked that how much you earn from daily catch? The daily catch varies from place to place and time to time. On an average the earning from daily catch is approximately Rs 500 to Rs 700 among the traditional fishers. And those who have mechanized boats get a larger amount, from Rs 3000 to Rs 7000 daily. There is no fixed income from the fish catch and many factors were responsible for the daily income from the catch. Here again the income of traditional fishers and the fishers who work in mechanized boats varies.

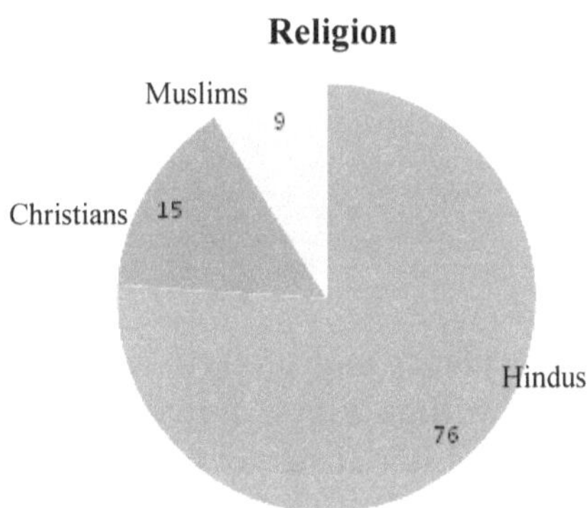

India's Maritime Security Interests

India has a coast line of 7516.60 Kms. There are nine States and four Union Territories that have coastal area. Though it is the duty of the Indian Navy and the Indian Coast Guard to provide the security of the maritime borders they cannot keep a constant vigil on the movement of men and materials along the entire coastal region. The Indian Navy is mainly stationed to the area beyond 200 nautical miles in international waters and Indian Coast Guard to look after the area from 12 nautical miles up to 200 nautical miles and the coastal police is responsible for the area up to 12 nautical miles from the shore. Therefore the coastal policing are necessary to supplement and not supplant the security responsibility of the Indian defence forces. It is also important to note that the coastal policing through coastal police stations alone cannot ensure a foolproof security arrangement in the coastal area or through the construction of fencing along the coastal area. Therefore the cooperation and support of the coastal community is sine quo non for the coastal security.

Coastal Security Agencies and their Mandate

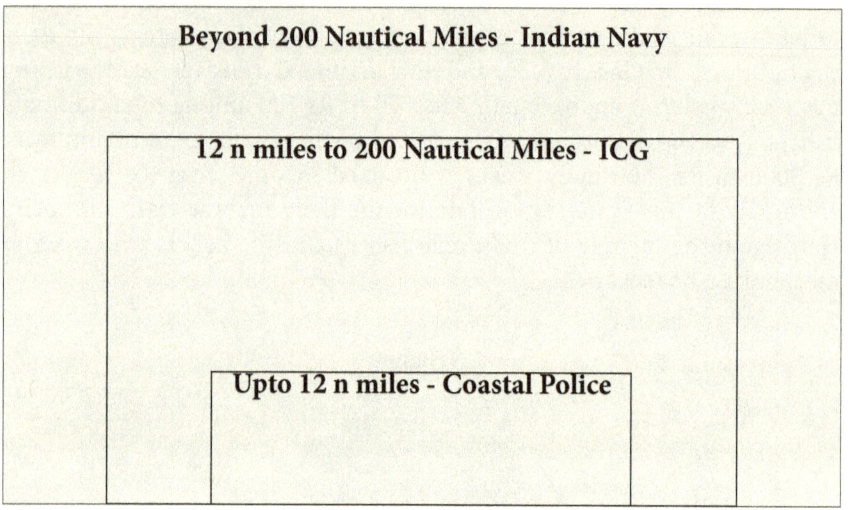

India has to step up surveillance and protection of India's vast coastline of 7,516.60 kms. India's maritime zones, over which it has certain rights and obligations, include a territorial sea up to 12 nm (22 kms) from the baseline, a contiguous zone from 12 to 24 nm (22-44 kms), an Exclusive Economic Zone (EEZ) from 12 to 200 nm (22-370 kms) and a continental shelf up to 200 nm. These zones currently comprise 2.013 million sq km area of sea which is the 12th largest in the world and equivalent to two-thirds of the total land area. India's has thousand-plus island territories and offshore installations. Again nearly 70 per cent of India's energy requirements of crude oil are currently shipped from abroad, increased focus would be required on the ability to maintain the safety and security of energy shipments and the prevention of any disruption of supply through multilateral cooperation. Another important maritime security interest of India is the prevention of maritime terrorism not only through multilateral efforts but also through comprehensive coastal security programme with the involvement of coastal community. (Annual Reports, MHA)

The task of providing security to the vast coastline, unlike the land borders, is a complex phenomenon involving multiple stake holders such as shipping, fisheries, offshore exploration and production, tourism, and scientific community. It is not only important to protect and promote the multifarious interests of different stake holders but also involve them in the coastal security programme.

Coastal Security and Maritime Security Agencies

There is currently a fragmentation of organizations, policies and legal and enforcement measures relating to maritime security issues. This results in overlapping of jurisdiction and inability to provide quick decisions or respond effectively to fast evolving situations. Currently, as many as 12 ministries and eight departments of the central government are involved in maritime-related policy formulation and implementation, as are nine coastal states and four union territories, with defence left to the Indian Navy and the Indian Coast Guard.

Governmental Agencies Involved in Coastal Security

1	Indian Navy
2	Indian Coast Guard
3	State Coastal Police
4	DG Lighthouses
5	Border Security Force & Lightships
6	Central Industrial Security Force
7	Port Trust
8	Intelligence Agencies
9	Other Armed Forces Shipping & Energy Operators
10	Customs and Immigration
11	DG Hydrocarbons
12	Economic Agencies
13	DG Shipping

Source: Annual Report 2017 -2018 MHA, GOI.

To deal with such a situation, a formal mechanism for coordination among the multiple users of the sea is urgently required. This would enable effective and time-urgent coordination among varied maritime related ministries/departments of the Government, as also the concerned states and union territories. In this respect, the Group of Ministers' report has recommended the formation of "an apex body for management of maritime affairs". Such an apex body would coordinate the activities of various agencies operating form different regions and having different mandates. The coastal security scheme is one such comprehensive initiative to address the problem of coastal security with the involvement of the coastal community.

Coastal Security Scheme and the role of Coastal Community

The Coastal Security Scheme has been formulated for strengthening infrastructure for patrolling and surveillance of country's coastal areas, particularly the shallow areas close to coast to check and counter illegal cross border activities and criminal activities using coast or sea. The Ministry of Home Affairs has been implementing Coastal Security Scheme in two phases (Phase-I -2005 to 2011 and Phase-II – 2011 – 2015). The scheme also aims at establishing institutional arrangements at state and district level for coordination among various agencies including the Indian Coast Guard and the IndianNavy.

The Coastal Security Scheme is under implementation in the nine coastal States and four coastal Union Territories since 2005. Under the scheme, in the first phase (2005-2011) assistance has been given to all the coastal states of Gujarat, Maharashtra, Goa, Karnataka, Kerala, Tamil Nadu, Andhra Pradesh, Orissa and West Bengal and the Union Territories of Daman & Diu, Lakshadweep, Puducherry and Andaman & Nicobar Islands to set up 73 coastal police stations 97 check posts 58 outposts. Under the Phase-II (2011 - 2015) of the Scheme it has been proposed to provide 131 Marine Police Stations, 60 jetties, 10 Marine Operation Centres (Annual Reports, MHA)

The proposal of the Phase-II Coastal Security Scheme has been formulated on the basis of vulnerability/gap analysis carried out by the coastal States and Union Territories in consultation with the Indian Coast Guard. The proposal was approved by the Government of India on 24 September 2010 for implementation from 1 April 2011 for a period of five years. The Scheme has provided support to coastal States/Union Territories to upgrade their coastal security apparatus. Nevertheless the task of securing

India's vast coastline is immense. There are 12 major ports and around 200 minor ports in the country. The 12 major ports are International Ship and Port Facility Security (ISPS) compliant and are subject to security audit once in two years. However, there is no such mechanism of security audit for the non-major ports. Apart from 12 major ports, 53 minor/non-major ports and 5 shipyards in the country are ISPS compliant.

As per the report of the home ministry of India a three tier coastal security ring all along India's coast is provided by Coastal Police, Indian Coast Guard and Indian Navy. Extensive surveillance and patrolling has been put into place across the Eastern and Western coastlines by the security forces in a coordinated manner. The Indian Coast Guard is undertaking extensive patrolling and surveillance along the eastern and western coast in coordination with other Central and State agencies viz Indian Navy, Coastal Police, Customs, CISF, Port Authority etc. Further, for effective surveillance, the deployment of assets by Indian Coast Guard in the Exclusive Economic Zone has been enhanced. On an average, every day about 18-20 ICG Ships are on patrol whereas about 8-10 aircrafts are on aerial surveillance sortie. At least one ship is being maintained on maritime borders with Pakistan and Sri Lanka. In addition, waters off Lakshadweep and Minicoy islands are maintained under constant surveillance during non- monsoon period by deployment of assets alternatively by Indian Coast Guard and Indian Navy.

Further Indian Coast Guard is conducting community interaction programmes in the fishing villages along the coast. The community interaction programmes are aimed at sensitizing the fishing community on the prevailing security situation and develop them to be the 'eyes and ears' for intelligence gathering. Thus the security agencies have well accepted the role of the coastal community in the coastal security scheme.

In this connection the proposal put forth by Professor K R Singh is an innovative step to gain the support of the coastal community in coastal security programme on a permanent basis. He had suggested the setting up of a Marine Guards on the lines of Home Guards by recruiting coastal people from each coastal locality. These trained Marine Guards would help the coastal security agencies in intelligence gathering which is a very vital input to the coastal security agencies to monitor the movement of men and materials along the vast coastal area. The gathering of intelligence through human being would also support the surveillance through electronic gadgets. This proposal if implemented will not only help to solve unemployment among coastal people but also help to enlist the support and cooperation of the coastal community in security related activities on a permanent basis. It is important to note that the Karnataka State has already selected 200 fishermen to be employed in coastal security police. Recently Tamil Nadu has also recruited coastal guards from the coastal community. The people from coastal villages can be recruited to the coastal police force as coastal guards and their seafaring experience is likely to be an asset to the security agencies.

In addition the coastal people can be trained to gather information which would support and supplement the necessary intelligence inputs to the marine police. India has a long coastal stretch and at several places the stretch lacks security forces. Hence, the fishermen if trained can be used to alert and inform in case they find anything unusual such as a person photographing or sketching, contacting ships with torch signals, transferring goods from a ship to a boat, transferring people, fisher folk fishing in areas not meant for fishing and are acting suspiciously or people urging fisher folk in buying their boats or renting them by paying a huge amount of money. One of the major problems with the new recruits in marine police is that they do not know the local language. Therefore it is necessary to concentrate on area-wise recruitment to coastal police. And through periodic awareness programme the coastal community can be trained to gather vital intelligence inputs to the security agencies. Thus when it came to protecting the coastal borders of the country, the fishing community could play a big role. In fact, every sea- faring fisherman can be trained to be a front man of coastal security.

Though there are periodic vulnerability/gap analyses, the Triton mock-drill, a coastal security exercises conducted by the Indian Navy had shown that terrorists could still find passages into the country through the sea. It has been pointed out that at one instance during the Triton exercise, "enemies" sent through the sea by the security agencies could bribe and gain entry into the country at one or two points. Therefore, there should be more awareness on coastal security. During this exercise it was also found that certain coastal area remained vigilant and the "terrorists" were captured with the cooperation of the fishing community. It shows that sea-faring fishermen were the eyes and ears of coastal security and no amount of modernized coastal security measures would equal them. As part of the coastal security programme, it had been decided to equip all categories of fishing vessels with radio-frequency identification gadgets. It would enable the security agencies to identify each and every fishing vessel out at sea. This, in turn, would enable checking of vessels without the gadget. Even then the fishing community would continue to be the vital aspect of coastal security.

The task of providing security to the vast coastline, unlike the land borders, is a complex phenomenon involving multiple stake holders. Among these stake holders the role of coastal community assumes significance in the coastal security programme. They are considered as the eye and ears of the coastal security. Now the question arise how to enlist the cooperation and support of the coastal community for effective coastal policing. Such support and cooperation are necessary on a permanent basis and round the clock. The cooperation and support of the coastal people are needed day in and day out to ensure coastal security. The livelihood for the fishing community comes from the sea. In this connection they also require protection from the security agencies involved in anti-piracy and related security operations of the defence forces.

In order to ensure the support of the coastal community it is important to build a better coastal community - police relations. Unlike other areas the coastal area is mainly occupied by the fishing community. Their problems are different from the problems of the people living in other area. Generally the coastal areas lag behind in basic amenities. This includes lack of safe drinking water, sanitation, proper housing, education, and other infrastructural facilities such as roads, hospitals, markets etc.

Since the livelihoods of the coastal community come from fishing it is difficult to relocate the coastal area settlers. As per the official reports about 5 million people are involved in fishing and related activities along the 156 coastal districts. There are 3,288 marine fishing villages and 1,511 marine fish landing centres in 9 maritime states and 2 union territories. The total marine fisher folk population was about 4 million comprising in 864,550 families. The whole hearted cooperation and support of the coastal community can be ensured only thorough improving the living conditions of the coastal people. The coastal community faces natural calamities such as sea erosion, tsunami etc. They are also the victims of climate change, pollution and poverty. In short the human security issues are numerous and imminent as far as the coastal community is concerned.

Thus when we look into the coastal security a convergence of the national security concerns and human security concerns is visible. The overall development of the coastal area would lead to better human security and better human security would result in enlisting the support of the coastal community in national security programme. Thus the development of infrastructural facilities in the coastal area not only improves the human security but also to enhance the coastal security and maritime security.

The security agencies in India had already maintained that the coastal community is the eyes and ears of coastal security. It is this understanding on the part of the security agencies which led to formal interaction between the coastal community and security agencies. The mass awareness drive has been initiated by the Indian Coast Guard in association with the department of fisheries at various location for the fishing community. The main objective of the drive was to re- emphasize the responsibility of fishing community towards the coastal security setup and their role as "Eyes and Ears" of the security agencies. This programme was also utilized to educate fishermen on safety and security aspects while operating at sea. Such interactions are beneficial to both the security agencies and the fishing community. It also enhances better police community relationship.

Coastal Community and Coastal Security

The security agencies have accepted that coastal communities are the largest constituents of the coastal security framework and are amongst its core strengths. They also claim that effective involvement of the vast four million strong fishing community, and the larger coastal community, has the potential to significantly complement efforts of the security agencies. The maritime security agencies will, therefore, foster the coastal community to serve as the 'eyes and ears' of security agencies. Community Interaction Programmes (CIP) are being conducted by the Indian Coast Guard at all fishing hamlets, to enhance awareness of the coastal community and fishermen in particular. However the survey carried out along the coastal India shows that there is scope for improving the CIP conducted by the Indian Coast Guard. Firstly, there is no regular periodicity in the conduct of such programme. In some areas it has been carried out in every three months whereas in some areas it is being conducted once in six months to one year. Secondly, the conduct of the class is not in the native language. And the fishing community found it very difficult to follow the lecture classes. Thirdly, the classes are often one sided and not of an interactive nature. (SureshR)

It is also observed that initiatives such as the 'Sagar Rakshak Dal' and Village Vigilance Committees, who are a voluntary group from fishing and coastal communities, assist the security agencies in surveillance, intelligence and patrolling, and have contributed to enhancing coastal security in several states. The toll free communication arrangements have been established, with shore-based control centres manned by State Coastal Police/Indian Coast Guard personnel in all states and Union Territories (UTs), in order to facilitate coastal community participation. These measures have not only improved security but have also saved lives, and provide an important link between fishermen and security agencies. Further the security agencies have also maintained that measures to involve, sensitize and incentivize the coastal community to contribute to the coastal security construct will remain a focus area. They also pointed out that implementation of Best Management Practices for security of vessels and offshore installations will also be promoted. There is also initiative towards issuing biometric identity card to the fishers and once this process is completed this will help the security agencies to monitor the identity of fishers with a card reader. Again color coding of the fishing vessels and installation of Automatic Identification System (AIS) in mechanized fishing boats is also in progress.

Again the coastal security projects have also envisaged the construction of coastal roads along the coastal areas and the development of infrastructural facilities. Such development along the coastal area would also promote coastal (beach) tourism. The development of tourism along the coastal area would also enhance the employment opportunities to the coastal people. One of the major problems before the coastal community is unemployment. This problem can be well addressed by development of tourism along the coastal area.

Thus particular attention needs to be paid to the maritime dimensions of national security as it is closely linked to India's political stability and economic prosperity. Concomitantly in the maritime security the coastal security aspect need to be focused. Along with enhancing the operational capabilities of the security agencies the problems of the coastal community also need to be addressed. A comprehensive programme needs to be initiated to address all aspects of coastal security with the active support of the coastal community. And the investments in the coastal security with the involvement of coastal people will not only enhance the national security but it also augments the human security.

The security audit report of Intelligence Bureau of last year found that out of 203 non- major/minor ports, 45 are non-operational while 75 have no security force. Further, many of these non-operational ports are used as fish landing points/jetties and this list includes 49 non- major ports. It also stated that out of the 49 non-major ports, 21 are located in Gujarat, nine in Maharashtra, five in Andhra Pradesh, two in Karnataka, 6 in Tamil Nadu, two in Puducherry and one each in Goa, Andaman and Nicobar islands,

Kerala and Odisha. It recommended several defence measures for effective coastal security and surveillance.

It appears that it is also important to strengthen the coastal community and coastal police relation for better coastal surveillance and security. It has long been recognized by the security agencies including the Indian navy that coastal community is the 'eyes' and 'ears' of coastal security matrix. Therefore the coastal infrastructure facilities need to be strengthened for better coastal security by incorporating the coastal area human resource development also in the coastal security scheme. Once the coastal area gets developed the coastal tourism also will be promoted which in turn enhance the economic development of these areas. Interestingly coastal security is an area where the national security and human security concerns converge.

There are many porous points along the vast coastal line. To prevent any infiltration of terrorists through the coast line a constant vigil along the coastal line is sine quo non. Such a task can be accomplished only with the whole hearted support from the fishing community. Thus the convergence of human security and national security concerns in the domain of coastal security once again point towards the imperatives of coastal community development programme and also a structural mechanism to enlist the support and cooperation of coastal community in ensuring a foolproof coastal security system.

References

Annual Reports of the Ministry of Home Affairs, Government of India 2017 – 2018 Annual Reports of the Ministry of External Affairs, Government of India 2017 – 2018 Annual Reports of the Ministry of Defence, Government of India 2017 – 2018

CMFRI, (2010) Marine Fisheries Census 2010 India, Ministry of Agriculture, GOI, 2010

Ensuring Secure Seas: India's Maritime Security Strategies, Indian Navy, Naval Strategic Publication (NSP) 1.2 October 2015 www.indiannavy.nic.in

Professor K R Singh (2013) Coastal Security- Maritime Dimensions of India's Homeland Security, Vij Publications, New Delhi.

Suresh R (2012) Peace in the Indian Ocean: A South Asian Perspective, Serials Publishers, New Delhi, ISBN: 9788183875059

Suresh R, (2013) India's Security Policy in the Post-Cold War Period in Prof. Mohanan B Pillai (Ed.) India's National Security Concerns and Strategies, New Century Publications, New Delhi 2013 ISBN 9788177083569

Suresh R, (2006) Human Security A Canadian Perspective, Holistic Thought, Vol. V No 1 & 2, Jan Dec 2006, .pp 103-113.

Suresh R, (2014) Maritime Security of India: The Coastal Security Challenges and Policy Options (Ed.) Vij Books India Pvt. Ltd. New Delhi 2014 ISBN: 9789382652366

Suresh R, (2015) The Changing Dimensions of Security: India's Security Policy Options, (Ed.) Vij Books India Pvt. Ltd. New Delhi, ISBN: 978-93-84464-80-6

Suresh R & Rakhee Viswambharan, (2014) Coastal Security of India: The Role of Coastal Community in Maritime Security of India: The Coastal Security Challenges and Policy Options (Ed.) Vij Books India Pvt. Ltd. New Delhi 2014 ISBN: 9789382652366

About The Editor

Dr Suresh R. is Professor, Department of Political Science, University of Kerala, Kariavattom Campus, Thiruvananthapuram, Kerala. He took M Phil degree in Political Science from University of Bombay, Mumbai and Ph D in International Studies from School of International Studies, Pondicherry Central University, Pondicherry, with UGC Junior Research Fellowship. He has published Five Books; *Foreign Policy and Human Rights: An Indian Perspective* (2009), *Peace in the Indian Ocean: A South Asian Perspective* (2011), *Right to Information and Good Governance* (2013), *Maritime Security of India: The Coastal Security Challenges and Policy Options* (2014), *The Changing Dimensions of Security and Indian's Security Policy Options* (2015) and contributed chapters to many books.

He had also published research articles in reputed National and International Journals. He had completed a UGC Major Research Project 'Maritime Security of India: The Coastal Security Challenges and Policy Options'. He has been selected as Associate in the Indian Institute of Advanced Study, Shimla and had completed a project on 'The Tibetan Issue and India - China Border Problem: A Security Perspective'. He is the Hon. Director of the prestigious V K Krishna Menon Study Centre for International Relations, University of Kerala, Thiruvananthapuram.

www.ingramcontent.com/pod-product-compliance
Lightning Source LLC
Chambersburg PA
CBHW020923160726
47993CB00005B/2101